# THE
# YANGZI
# RIVER

Judy Bonavia

Revised by William Hurst

D0910934

 **PASSPORT BOOKS**

Trade Imprint of National Textbook Company
Lincolnwood, Illinois U.S.A.

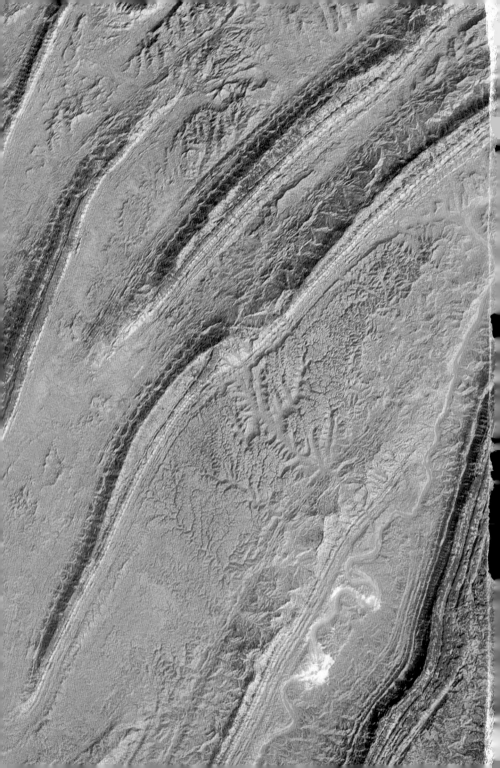

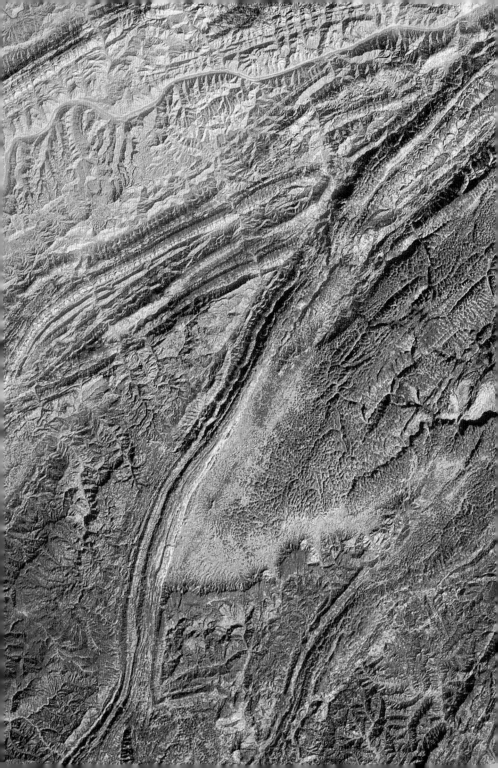

*(preceding page) GEOPIC™ image of the Yangzi in eastern Sichuan*
*(right) Tibetan road worker at rest*

Published by Passport Books in conjunction with
The Guidebook Company Ltd.

This edition first published in 1989 by Passport Books, Trade
Imprint of National Textbook Company, 4255 West Touhy
Avenue, Lincolnwood (Chicago), Illinois 60646-1975 U.S.A.

Printed in Hong Kong

'Autumn Thoughts,' by C. H. Wang, translated by Wu-chi Liu from *Sunflower Splendor*,
copyright © 1975 by Wu-chi Liu and Irving Yucheng Lo. 'A Boatman's Song' by Wang
Chien, translated by William H. Nienhauser from *Sunflower Splendor*,
copyright © William H. Nienhauser. Reprinted by permission of Doubleday &
Company, Inc.

Series Editors: May Holdsworth and Sallie Coolidge

Photography by GEOPIC™ (2–3) © Earth Satellite Corporation, Jacky Yip (5, 6,
12–13, 14–15, 16–17, 18–19, 20, 23, 25, 34–35, 38, 56–57, 91, 102–103); Tom
Nebbia (28–29, 46, 67, 70–71, 74–75, 78–79, 86, 98, 106, 118–119, 122–123, 143,
164); Caroline Courtauld (66, 82, 87, 111); Paddy Booz (52, 61, 99, 114–115, 161);
Sydney Wong (39); Wang Gang Feng (151, 160); Anthony Cassidy (130–131, 134);
Ingrid Morejohn (139); Alfred Ko (147); R. Wada (49).

Design by Rican Design Associates

# Contents

The name of the river described in this guide is romanized in several ways; the most widely adopted forms are Yangtze and Yangtse. The official *pinyin* spelling, Yangzi, has been adopted for this book. Other names and addresses are also rendered in *pinyin*. *Dajie*, *dadao* and *da malu* are main thoroughfares; *lu* and *jie* are respectively roads and streets; *long* and *xiang* are lanes or alleys.

# The River's Source

*A Photographic Essay*

From the bitter cold and treeless alps of Upper Qinghai, around the source of the Yangzi, the snow that gradually melts in the summer sun trickles down the beds of ancient glaciers, and finally reaches the pastures where man and beast can survive. The snowmelt forms small streams which sing through the tilted plateaus and nourish the grass-roots and the hardy little flowers and plants which the local Tibetan people use as medicine for a variety of ills.

The streams flow more swiftly down the lower Qinghai mountains, which give an impression of Central Europe. On successive steps of mountain and plateau, the people of the Yushu Tibetan Autonomous District cultivate barley and shelter the herds in the winter, sending them up to the high pastures only in spring. Their diet consists of meat, milk (fresh and fermented), and barley-meal, which is the staple. Sometimes they add sugar brought from distant parts of China. And in the forest belts they cut timber for the construction of new towns.

The ubiquitous yak is the most useful beast, but sheep are reared for meat and wool and there are some goats. The tough, shaggy little ponies of the mountains are used as a means of transport, and mares' milk is a treasured delicacy and cure-all.

Animal husbandry is the main occupation of these Tibetans and they continue to lead a semi-nomadic life, living in thick black yak-hair tents lined with bags of precious barley, and surrounded by their grazing flocks. For several days each spring the people gather together to sing, dance, hold horse-races and tugs of war, before again returning to their lives of isolation.

The streams turn to sizeable rivers as they come down to the 3,000-metre (10,000-foot) level or thereabouts. Typically they flow blue and wide across valley floors where the barley is now fairly abundant and small villages — decorated with the inevitable Buddhist prayer flags — take the place of tent encampments. Despite their deep poverty, the women dress gaily in black and a rainbow of decorative colours, plaiting their hair almost like Africans, and wearing it in braids, sometimes interwoven with red cord. To commemorate special religious festivals, pilgrimages are made to monasteries (often many days' riding away) for they are social as well as religious occasions.

The wildlife is abundant — Tibetan antelopes, Mongolian gazelles, snow leopards, otters, martens, lynxes and deer as well as dozens of species of birds. Carp throng the cold waters of the lakes. Nature reserves are being established to protect the environs of the beautiful threatened snow leopard and the primeval forests in which the wild ass and the snow cock still roam.

# The Course of the Yangzi

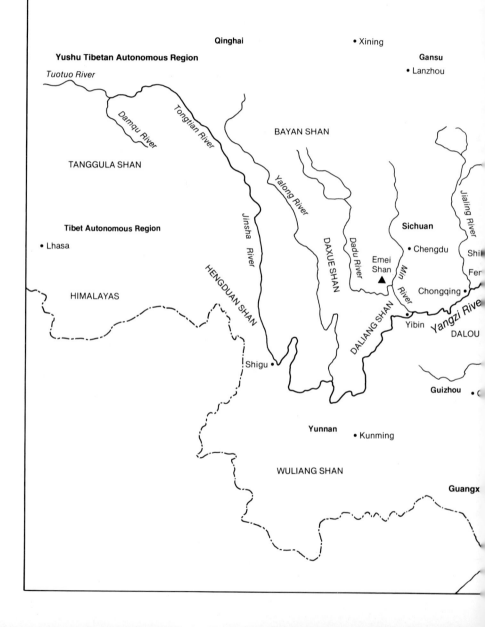

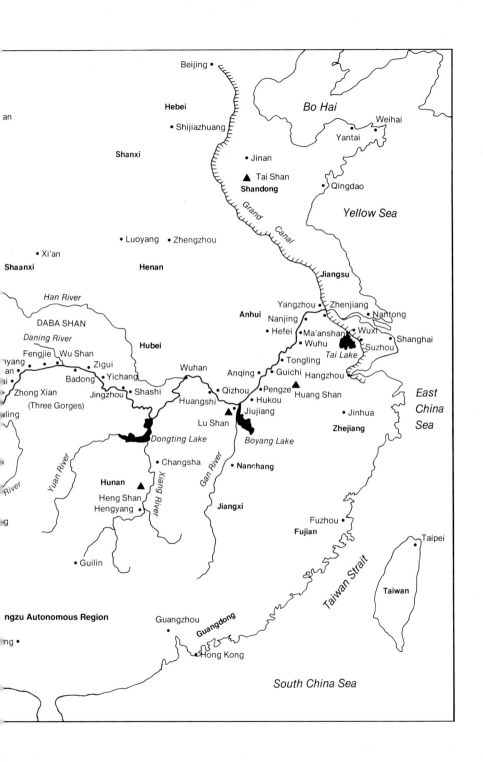

*Source of the Yangzi, Qinghai – Tibetan border*

*Yaks transporting timber, eastern Tibet*

*Fields of barley, near Dege*

# Getting There

Chongqing in Sichuan Province is the normal starting point for the downriver Yangzi cruises. Boat departures are normally early in the morning so it is usually necessary to spend the night in Chongqing. The journey through the Three Gorges to Yichang and on downstream to Wuhan takes three and a half days, while the upriver journey, from Wuhan to Chongqing, takes four and a half days.

**Scheduled Passenger Boats** Regular passenger boats (*ban chuan*) travel all the way to Shanghai. However, it should be noted that most of these boats terminate at either Yichang or Wuhan, and it is therefore necessary to book onward passages at these stops. There are ticket offices at the piers. Depending on the type of boat and its schedule, the 1,125-kilometre (700-mile) journey between Wuhan and Shanghai may take up to four days upstream and three days downstream.

There are daily sailings of these scheduled passenger boats in both directions from Wuhan, Nanjing and Shanghai. They serve all the Yangzi towns and indeed, for many of these towns, the boats are the only viable means of long-distance transport, since the ports are not all connected by motorable roads. Fares vary with the distance travelled.

The largest passenger shipping line operating on the Yangzi, the Golden Line (previously known as the Dongfanghong or East is Red Company), has a number of boats which carry over 1,200 passengers. The accommodation is divided into five classes. The best and most expensive is second-class, which consists of two-berth compartments furnished with bedding, two thermos flasks, a desk and two armchairs, with adjacent hot and cold washing facilities. On some boats there is also a communal sitting room for viewing. The third-class section provides ten-person accommodation in two-tiered bunks; the fourth is similar, with bunks for 12 or more persons; and in the fifth class passengers are packed into masses of three-tiered bunks. In addition, many passengers buy a ride with no sleeping accommodation and just squeeze into what available space they can find in the gangways and other public areas of the boat. All the boats have basic dining rooms and the times for meals are announced during the journey. Hot water is always available from a tap located somewhere on the boat — just follow any passenger who looks as if he is about to make tea or instant noodles in his all-purpose enamel mug.

**Cruise Boats** In recent years tourists have been taking special cruise boats which ply the Chongqing–Wuhan stretch. The boats operate from the end of March or the beginning of April to October or November. During the height of the tourist season it is extremely difficult to obtain boat tickets on this scenic run. Most of the boats are booked up by groups well in advance of the season, but individual travellers can try for tickets at short notice in case there are cancellations.

The cruise is normally three days downstream and four days upstream. Yichang is rapidly becoming a popular terminal point for these cruises.

Since the Three Gorges cruise is one of the most widely promoted and popular tours for foreign visitors to China, the various tourism-related authorities are pushing to get more boats built. At present there are 11 cruise boats: the *Goddess* (*Shennu*), the *Kunlun*, the *Yangtzekiang*, the *Three Gorges* (*Sanxia*), the *Emei*, the *Bashan*, the *White Emperor* (*Baidi*), the *Great Wall* (*Changcheng*), the *Merchant Princess* (*Longzhong*), the *Xiling* and the *Yangtse Star* (*Changjiang Zhi Xing*). They vary in size from a relatively small boat like the *Kunlun*, which has 18 twin cabins, to the *Great Wall*, with nearly a hundred. They are all comfortably appointed and air-conditioned, and most cabins come with attached showers or bathrooms. In addition to observation decks, lounges, bars and dining rooms, the larger ships also offer swimming pools, ballrooms, currency exchange counters, gift shops, hairdressers and clinics.

## Getting to Chongqing

**By Air** Southwest Airlines (a regional arm of Civil Aviation Administration of China) has introduced a scheduled international flight weekly (on Thursdays) from Hong Kong. Within China, there are daily flights from Beijing, Shanghai and Canton (Guangzhou). It is also possible to reach Chongqing by air from Changsha, Chengdu, Guilin, Kunming, Nanjing, Wuhan and Xi'an.

**By Rail** Chongqing is accessible by train from all major cities in China, with changes where appropriate. The most common routes are from Kunming via Chengdu, Guilin via Guiyang, and by a direct service from Beijing.

## Getting to Yichang

**By Air** Flights to Yichang operate daily from Wuhan, three times a week from Beijing (via Zhengzhou), twice-weekly from Shanghai, and twice-weekly from Canton (via Changsha).

The air network has been supplemented by China Tourism Charter Air-Service Company (with an agency in Yichang) which arranges charter flights to some 18 cities from Dangyang Air Field. CITS is the best source for information on these flights.

**By Rail** Trains run several times daily between Yichang and Wuhan.

## Getting to Wuhan

**By Air** As the provincial capital of Hubei, Wuhan is an important centre in the transport network of central China, but at present it is served by only one international flight — the chartered service on CAAC to and from Hong Kong on Thursdays. Daily domestic flights connect Wuhan with major Chinese cities such as Beijing, Shanghai and Canton.

**By Rail** Wuhan is 18 hours from Beijing and about 24 hours from Canton. There are also direct trains between Wuhan and Yichang, Chengdu, Xi'an, Tianjin, Qingdao, Guilin and Zhangjiang.

# Climate and Clothing

The three large cities along the Yangzi River — Chongqing, Wuhan and Nanjing — are known traditionally as the 'three furnaces of China'. Between April and September, the temperature in the Yangzi River valley reaches 36°C (97°F) and above. Spring and autumn are therefore the best seasons for making the river cruises. However, with the tall mountains and gorges through which the river threads its path, precipitation is very high and the peaks are often shrouded in cloud and mist, although a light haze can enhance the beauty of the scenery. Summer rains are torrential and dramatic thunderstorms are comforting if you are on board your boat but a nuisance should you be trying to sightsee ashore. The winters are short, cold and crisp.

Late summer travellers will coincide with the high-water periods, when the river rises swiftly, almost perceptibly. For the rest of the year, tourists will find the water level lower.

Light summer clothing is all that is required between April and September, with a woollen cardigan or warm jacket for the cool evenings on board. Those who rise at dawn to watch the passage through the gorges may imitate the Chinese passengers who huddle in blankets supplied by the ship.

The Yangzi River towns are very informal indeed; wear comfortable everyday clothes when you visit them. Steep steps from the jetties to the towns require walking shoes, and since the streets turn to mud within minutes of a heavy rainfall, you may need an extra pair. Umbrellas can be bought cheaply almost anywhere.

Warm clothes are essential for the river journeys during seasons other than summer. The boats can be draughty and the wind piercing.

# The Yangzi River: an Introduction

The mighty Yangzi, or Changjiang, is the third largest river in the world. (The Amazon is the longest, followed by the Nile.) The Yangzi at 6,300 kilometres (3,900 miles) is closest in length to the Mississippi. Among the Chinese, the name Yangzi is not as commonly used as Changjiang — simply, Long River.

This extensive waterway cuts through the heart of China, and is regarded by the Chinese as marking the division of their country into north and south, both geographically and culturally. The river rises in the far western part of China and flows through eight provinces before disgorging its waters into the Yellow Sea. Over 700 tributaries draining a further six provinces join the Yangzi along its course.

The Yangzi is divided into three parts:

**The Upper Reaches** from the source in Qinghai Province to Yichang in Hubei Province, a distance of some 4,400 kilometres (2,700 miles). This stretch is one of great beauty, with wild mountain ranges, unbroken ravines, unnavigable rapids and rushing torrents. The Three Gorges are included in this section, as is the Sichuan Basin.

**The Middle Reaches** from Yichang to Hukou at the mouth of Boyang Lake in Jiangxi Province, a distance of about 1,000 kilometres (620 miles). Here, the river widens and flows through flat, low-lying

land and is fed by waters from two huge lakes, the Dongting and the Boyang. This is the region where the battle against flooding has been carried on for centuries; earthen dikes and paved embankments tell of past and present heroic struggles.

**The Lower Reaches** from Hukou to the estuary, a distance of some 900 kilometres (560 miles). The landscape in the river's lower course is typified by a flat delta plain crisscrossed by canals and waterways, with soil so rich and water so abundant that the region has been known for centuries as the 'Land of Fish and Rice'.

The wet season begins in April, bringing heavy rain in the middle and lower reaches. By July and August the wet weather reaches the Sichuan Basin where the prevalence of mountainous terrain causes widespread rainfall. Then, as the water level starts to subside, the 'Sichuan waters' begin to threaten again.

The rich Yangzi River Basin, according to current statistics, produces 40% of the national grain (including 70% of all paddy rice), one-third of the country's cotton, 48% of its freshwater fish and 40% of the total industrial output value. Its hydroelectric energy potential is almost boundless: when the Gezhouba Dam (a hydropower and water conservancy project) is completed (1988) it will be one of the biggest low-water dams in the world. One-third of China's 1.1 billion people live in this prosperous basin, which also boasts a rich cultural heritage.

One would imagine from the impressive statistics that the river would be choked with vessels of all descriptions, but this is not the case. Ocean-going ships do frequent the river from Wuhan down, but the traffic consists mainly of ferry boats, lighters, barges, tugs and logging rafts. Over the years, political instability had taken its toll on economic development, but it was the building of railways in the hinterland that really changed the life of the river. When rail freight proved to be cheaper than transportation along the Yangzi and its tributaries, the heyday of river transport was over.

Attempts are being made to revitalize the river transport system. Studies point out that it is cheaper to dredge than to build branch railways. Over three billion *yuan* of state investment has been fed into the Yangzi shipping industry in the last 35 years.

## Yangzi River's Main Tributaries

| River | Length | | Drainage Area | | Rate of Flow at Mouth | |
|---|---|---|---|---|---|---|
| | *Kilometres* | *(Miles)* | *Square kilometres* | *(Square miles)* | *Cubic metres per second* | *(Cubic yards per second)* |
| Yalong | 1,187 | (738) | 144,280 | (55,690) | 2,000 | (2,620) |
| Min | 793 | (493) | 133,570 | (51,560) | 3,040 | (3,980) |
| Jialing | 1,119 | (695) | 159,810 | (61,690) | 2,000 | (2,620) |
| Wu | 1,018 | (633) | 88,220 | (34,050) | 1,750 | (2,290) |
| Yuan | 993 | (617) | 89,960 | (34,720) | 2,460 | (3,220) |
| Xiang | 811 | (504) | 92,500 | (35,700) | 2,400 | (3,140) |
| Han | 1,532 | (952) | 174,350 | (67,300) | 1,690 | (2,210) |
| Gan | 758 | (471) | 81,660 | (31,520) | 2,590 | (3,390) |

# Boats Great and Small

The traditional Chinese boats which navigated the Yangzi were *sanpans* (meaning three planks), the larger-sized *wupans* (five planks) and junks. Their sails were tall to capture any welcome breeze, and stiffened by bamboo battens. The sculling oar, or *yuloh*, was extremely long with normally four men working it. Mats overhead provided shelter for passengers; decks were covered with coils of bamboo rope. Local pilots were hired to negotiate the most difficult rapids. Their instructions were relayed to the harnessed trackers pulling the long hauling ropes — often far ahead of the boat — by a drum beaten at different rhythms. Large freight junks often required three or four hundred trackers as well as groups of strong swimmers who would loosen the ropes should they snag on rocks along the way.

An eighth-century poem gives a compelling picture of the gruelling drudgery of a boat puller's life:

> *A Boatman's Song*
> Oh, it's hard to grow up at the way-station side!
> The officials've set me to pullin' station boats;
> Painful days are more, happy days are few,
> Slippin' on water, walkin' on sand, lake birds of the sea;
> Against the wind, upstream, a load of ten thousand bushels —
> Ahead, the station's far away; behind, it's water everywhere!
> Midnight on the dikes, there's snow and there's rain,
> From up top our orders: you still have to go again!
> Our clothes are wet and cold beneath our short rain cloaks,
> Our hearts're broke, our feet're split, how can we stand the pain?
> Till break of dawn we suffer, there's no one we can tell,
> With one voice we trudge along, singing as we pull;
> A thatch-roofed house, what's it worth,
> When we can't get back to the place of our birth!
> I would that this river turn to farm plots,
> And long may we boatmen stop cursing our lots.
>
> Wang Qian (768–833)

They were truly beasts of burden, as observed by an American, William L. Hall, and his wife, who spent several weeks on a small Chinese cargo-boat in 1922:

If the boat happens to turn about when it is struck by a cross-current, a call from the pilot brings all the trackers to their knees or makes them dig their toes into the dirt. Another call makes them either claw the earth or catch their fingers over projecting stones. Then they stand perfectly still to hold the boat. When it is righted, another call makes them let up gradually and then begin again their hard pull.

Passengers usually took 'kuaize' — large *wupans* — and paid for the Yichang−Chongqing trip 185 cash for every 100 *li* (18 cents for every 50 kilometres, or 30 miles). They would also supply wine for the crew, and incense and fireworks for a propitious journey. Going upriver, this journey used to take as long as 40−50 days in the high-water period and 30 days in low water, depending on the size of the boat, while the downriver trip could be completed in 5−12 days. At the end of the journey the passengers might buy some pork as a feast for the crew.

River life was varied along the Yangzi and its tributaries. Big junks, fitted out as theatres, sailed between the towns to give performances of Chinese opera or juggling. Some boats were built as hotels, offering accommodation to travellers arriving too late at night to enter the city gates. Others were floating restaurants and teahouses, not to mention boats which were a source of livelihood as well as home to the numerous fisherfolk and their families.

Peasants along the lower and middle Yangzi first set eyes on foreign men-of-war and steamers when Britain's Lord Elgin journeyed as far as Wuhan (Hankow) in 1842. Although the Chinese had in fact invented the paddle wheel (worked probably by the treadmill system) for driving their battleships as early as the eighth century, paddle boats were not widely used. In an incident on Dongting Lake in 1135, they were proved positively useless when the enemy threw straw matting on the water and brought the paddle wheels to a stop. They seem not to have been used since.

With the opening up of the Yangzi ports to foreign trade in the latter half of the 19th century, foreign shallow draught paddle steamers and Chinese junks worked side by side. But the traditional forms of river transport slowly became obsolete, and were confined to the Yangzi tributaries for transporting goods to the distribution centres.

Early Western shipping on the Shanghai−Wuhan stretch of the river was dominated by Americans, whose experience of paddle steamers on the Mississippi and other rivers had put them to the fore. The American firm of Russell and Company was the leading shipping and trading concern in those years. A fifth of the foreign trade was in opium shipped up to Wuhan. By the late 1860s, British companies such as Jardine & Matheson and Butterfield & Swire had successfully challenged the American supremacy. Accommodation on the companies' river boats was luxurious, and trade was brisk.

The Wuhan−Yichang stretch was pioneered by an English trader, Archibald Little, who established a regular passenger service in 1884 with his small steamer *Y-Ling*. In his book *Through the Yang-tse Gorges*, he described the bustling scene on the river:

The lively cry of the trackers rings in my ears, and will always be associated in my mind with the rapids of the Upper Yang-tse. This cry is 'Chor-Chor', said to mean 'Shang-chia', or 'Put your shoulder to it', 'it' being the line which is slung over the shoulder of each tracker, and attached to the quarter-mile-long towrope of plaited bamboo by a hitch, which can be instantaneously cast off and rehitched. The trackers mark time with this cry, swinging their arms to and fro at each short step, their bodies bent forward, so that their fingers almost touch the ground. . . . Eighty or a hundred men make a tremendous noise at this work, almost drowning the roar of the rapids, and often half a dozen junks' crews are towing like this, one behind the other. From the solemn stillness of the gorge to the lively commotion of a rapid, the contrast is most striking.

Other companies soon followed, but none dared travel this route at night. Again, it was Archibald Little's perseverance that brought about steamship navigation through the gorges above Yichang to Chongqing. Acting as captain and engineer, he successfully navigated his 17-metre (55-foot) *Leechuan* up to Chongqing in 1898, though he still needed trackers to pull him over the worst rapids.

During the heyday of the Yangzi in the 1920s and 1930s, travel by steamer from Shanghai all the way up to Chongqing was luxurious though not entirely safe. Halfway, at Wuhan, passengers had to change to smaller boats for the rest of the journey.

After the establishment of the People's Republic of China, emphasis was placed on making the Yangzi safe for navigation all year round. and all the major obstructions were blown up.

The Yangzi today is still a vital artery. Many river towns are almost entirely dependent on it for connecting them to each other. The regular ferries and boats, offering a range of accommodation, always overflow with passengers (see page 21). There are also luxury cruise boats which normally ply the Chongqing–Wuhan stretch, for three days downstream and four upstream. There are now 11 of these cruise boats, carrying between 36 and 180 passengers, and more will be put into service in the next few years.

The captains of the Yangzi passenger boats must serve ten years' apprenticeship before being given their own command.

# The Upper Reaches

The melting glaciers and snow fields of the rugged Tanggula Mountains in Qinghai Province form the headwaters of the Yangzi. It is only since 1976 that the river's true source, the 6,621-metre (21,700-foot) high Mount Geladandong, on the Qinghai–Tibet Plateau, has been conclusively explored and surveyed.

The source of this greatest of China's rivers had long been a geographical conundrum. The area is largely in permafrost, moraine pitted and wind-swept, an inhospitable and discouraging environment for explorers. A treatise written in the Warring States period (475–221 BC) by geographer Yu Gong stated the source to be in the Mingshan Mountains of Sichuan Province. By the 16th century, explorers had named Jingsha River in Qinghai as the headstream. In the first half of the 18th century, an official Qing government expedition found its way to the Qinghai–Tibet Plateau; their reports were an impetus for further explorations. But it was only when the Changjiang Valley Planning Office sent forth a scientific investigative team in the mid-1970s that the source was finally ascertained.

As the snows melt in the short summer months, waters quietly trickle down to the foothills and flow through the marshes and lakes that form the plateau with its freshly verdant grassland. Among the many rivulets in this region, the Tuotou River emerges as the main body of water, winding its way towards the Qinghai–Tibet Highway and eastwards, for a further 60 kilometres (37 miles), where it is joined by the Damqu River. At this point it becomes the broad upper reaches of the Tongtian River. This plateau abounds in wildlife: Tibetan antelope, wild yaks and asses, lynx and geese.

The 813-kilometre (505-mile) Tongtian River, descending sharply, flows through the Yushu Tibetan Autonomous Region of Qinghai, where the flatlands are cultivated for highland barley or *qingke* — the Tibetan staple diet — and hillslopes provide grazing for the yak, sheep and white-lipped deer owned by Tibetan herdsmen whose dwellings are black, yak-wool tents. Below the Yushu region the river, navigable here only for short distances by skin coracle boats, becomes known as the Jinsha (Golden Sand) River and flows southwards, forming the border between Tibet and Sichuan on a 2,308-kilometre (1,434-mile) journey sweeping down into Yunnan Province and looping back up into Sichuan. On this southward sweep the Yangzi runs parallel to the upper reaches of the Mekong and Salween Rivers (both of which also rise in the high plateau of Tibet) and the eastern branch of the Irrawaddy. At Shigu (Stone Drum) in Yunnan, the river curves sharply north, actually flowing parallel to itself, separated by only 24

kilometres (15 miles). Here the river is wide in summer, but in winter, when the water level is low, the currents form sandbars which become the breeding grounds for many varieties of waterbirds. Further on the river again plunges south and east and eventually northwards unrelentingly towards Chongqing.

This southern region of the river is an area few Westerners have ever penetrated. In the second half of the 19th century, the British and French, from their colonial possessions in Burma, Laos and Vietnam, sought to establish back-door trade routes through Yunnan and up to the navigable stretches of the Yangzi in Sichuan. Secret missions were sent into southwest China, as the British were anxious to study the feasibility of a railway link between Burma and Chongqing. It was these intrepid travellers (some of whom never lived to tell their tale) who recorded their encounters with the many tribal minority peoples inhabiting this area. Western missionaries were a second source of information on customs and attitudes. But the first Westerner to explore and photograph the area extensively was an American, Joseph F. Rock, leader of the National Geographic Society's Yunnan Province Expedition. His amazing black and white photographs, taken in the 1920s and developed by himself under the most difficult conditions, are, even today, outstanding.

Among the sloping forests of pine and spruce are alpine meadows of moss, blue gentians and white edelweiss bordered by hemlock and flowering rhododendron bushes. In the narrow valley floors live tribes of the Tibeto-Burmese ethnic group — the Lisu, Nashi, Lolo (also known as the Yi), Nosu, Lahu, Hsifan and Jing peoples. They have inhabited western Sichuan and northeast Yunnan since earliest times, cultivating barley, wheat, vegetables and indigo and keeping sheep or pigs. For the most part these people are Tibetan Buddhists, but some, like the Nashi, are animists whose priests or *tombas* practise exorcism in the pre-Buddhist tradition of the Bon sect of Tibet; others are simply shamanistic. They are brave hunters and warriors, who had fought amongst themselves and against the Han Chinese for centuries. Banditry was commonplace. Until 1949, Buddhist kingdoms, such as the tiny kingdom of Muli, were ruled by reincarnated monk kings.

The Black Yi of Daliang Shan were landowners who kept their fellow tribesmen, the White Yi, as slaves. This practice was proscribed in 1956. The Yi — in their striking long thick black capes — were a constant headache to the Chinese administration, as they kidnapped officials and fomented rebellions. Their exploits were recorded as early as the first century BC by the great Chinese historian Sima Qian (*c.* 145–85 BC). Kublai Khan (1215–94), in an attempt to bring Burma under his sway, lost half his 500,000-man army to disease, exhaustion and tribal harassment in these mountains.

Though the great gorges of the Yangzi near Yichang are the most famous, there are even more spectacular gorges in the vicinity of Lijiang, where mountains rise more than 5,700 metres (18,700 feet) and canyons plunge 3,900 metres (12,800 feet) through which the water flows deeply, turbulently and treacherously. Access in this region is still only by mountain pathways and cliff-hugging tracks. Single-rope bridges slung high above the water's surface are not uncommon; the rider is conveyed in a sling attached to a pulley which must be well greased with yak butter to avoid any buildup of friction.

The area is rich in mineral resources and timber. The 1,085-kilometre (675-mile) long Chengdu−Kunming railway (constructed in the 1970s) has brought profound changes to this remote region.

From about the 27 degrees north parallel, the Yangzi, flowing north-northeast for some 800 kilometres (500 miles) and forming the borders of Sichuan and Yunnan, finally reaches the Sichuan or Red Basin. At Yibin, the river, now called the Changjiang, is joined by the Minjiang and Tuojiang Rivers from the north and the Wujiang from the south. Thus originates the name of Sichuan Province — 'Four Rivers'. The 500-metre (1,640-foot) high Sichuan Basin, with its mild winters and long rainy season, has long been agriculturally rich: in the late Han Dynasty, Chengdu (today's capital of Sichuan) was even bigger than the capital of Luoyang. Sichuan has remained one of China's most important 'bread-baskets', producing cotton, hemp and silk as well as grain. On the large flat Chengdu plain, the Minjiang was harnessed for irrigation as early as 250 BC by the Dujiangyan irrigation system, which has been the basis of the region's prosperity ever since.

Near the confluence of the Dadu and Min Rivers is the great sacred Buddhist mountain of Emei, studded with ancient temples. Not far distant, at Leshan, the river actually laps the stone feet of one of the world's largest carved Buddhas. The 70-metre (230-foot) high Tang-Dynasty (618−907) statue took 90 years to complete.

The huge city of Chongqing stands at the confluence of the Jialing and the Yangzi. Below this city the river continues its progress through Sichuan, and on through the famous Yangzi Gorges into Hubei Province where, at Yichang, sharply checked by the Gezhouba Dam, it enters the flatlands of its middle reaches.

## Chongqing

The hilltop city of Chongqing, surrounded on three sides by water, is a large industrial city and a crucial centre in the transport infrastructure of southwestern China. It is also the embarkation point for cruises through the famous Three Gorges and on down to Wuhan or

Shanghai. Today the city has a population of about 14 million, making it the largest city in China.

There is a striking lack of bicycles — ubiquitous in other Chinese cities — for not only is the city built on rolling hills, but it is also one of the hottest places in China, classified, along with Wuhan and Nanjing, as one of the country's 'three furnaces'. From mid-June the citizens take their rattan beds out into the streets at night in order to gain some relief from the steamy summer temperatures of up to 40°C (104°F).

## *History of Chongqing*

In the fourth century BC, Chongqing (then called Yuzhou) was the capital of the State of Ba, whose men were renowned for their prowess in battle and their military successes. In the Southern Song Dynasty (1127–1279) the city's name was changed to Chongqing — meaning 'double celebration' — to mark the princedom and enthronement of Emperor Zhaodun in 1189. He was himself a native of the city.

Chongqing had always been an important port, bustling with junks from Sichuan's hinterlands and neighbouring provinces, and acting as the collection point for the abundant produce of the region — hides

and furs from Tibet, hemp, salt, silk, rhubarb, copper and iron. Under the Qifu Agreement of 1890, Chongqing was opened to foreign trade. This marks the beginning of the exciting history of steamboat navigation from Yichang through the treacherous gorges to Chongqing, a development aimed at opening up the riches of Sichuan to trade with the outside world. By the early part of this century, abetted by warlord factionalism and greed, a massive trade in opium grown in southwest China had sprung up.

Visitors to the city in the 1920s and '30s commented on its 30-metre (100-foot) high city wall, and the rough steps from the river up to the city gates 'dripping with slime from the endless procession of water-carriers'. At that time, Chongqing, with a population of over 600,000, had no other water supply. Between ten and twenty thousand coolies carried water daily to shops and houses through the steep and narrow lanes of the city. All porterage was done by coolies as there were no wheeled vehicles in the city, only sedan chairs.

In 1939, during the Sino-Japanese War, the Guomindang (Nationalist) government of China moved the capital from Nanjing to Chongqing, and on the south bank of the Yangzi foreign legations built substantial quarters, which can be seen from the river. The airstrip used then can still be seen on the Penghu Sandbar as one crosses the Yangzi River Bridge. The Guomindang government headquarters is now the People's City Government Offices (only the gateway is left of that period), situated just opposite the Renmin Hotel.

During the Sino-Japanese War (1937–45), Chongqing's notorious weather conditions probably saved the city from complete devastation, for only on clear days could the Japanese bombers, which flew over in 20-minute waves, succeed in dropping their thousands of bombs.

## What to See in Chongqing

Chongqing, always a trading city, was never noted for its cultural heritage or architecture. Unlike northern Chinese cities, Chongqing and other Yangzi River towns are very lively at night. On summer evenings residents stroll about in the hope of a refreshing breeze. Street markets, sidewalk restaurant stalls, herbalists and calligraphers can be found on Wuyi Lu and Bayi Lu. Informal Sichuanese opera can be heard at the **Workers' Park** on Saturday evenings.

There are two cable-car crossings of the 736-metre (800-yard) wide Jialing River, one at Jinyangmen and another at Wanglongmen.

The **Chongqing Zoo** has four pandas, which are native to Sichuan Province.

**Liberation Tower**
This structure on Minzu Lu forms the centre of the downtown area. It was built in 1945 to commemorate the end of the Second World War.

**Pipa Hill**
Pipa Hill, the highest point of the city, is an ideal spot to view the city lights in the evening. Before 1949 it was the grounds of a warlord's residence, but it was turned into a public park in 1955.

**Goose Peak Park**
This park to the west is dotted with traditional-style pavilions, ponds and gardens. Established in 1909, it was for some time the summer house of a rich local salt-merchant; the original buildings have been destroyed and the current pavilions date from a more recent period.

**Chongqing Museum and Natural History Museum**
There is an interesting collection of exhibits here, at 72 Pipashan Zhengjie, including a large display of Eastern Han-Dynasty (25–220) stone carvings found in Sichuan. Of particular interest are the two huge, 2,000-year old black wooden 'boat' coffins (and the artifacts found inside them) which were suspended from cliffs by the Ba people, the earliest inhabitants of Sichuan. The Natural History Museum houses a dinosaur's skeleton found in Zigong County.

**Red Rock Villa and Gui Yuan**
Both these are now memorial museums to the 1949 revolutionary activities in the city. In the 1930s and '40s, during the period of cooperation between the Guomindang government and the Chinese Communist Party against the aggression of the Japanese, these buildings were the offices of the Communist Party and the Red Army.

**South Mountains Park (Nanshan Gongyuan)**
Situated on the southern side of the Yangzi, this park comprises a scenic group of five mountain peaks between 400 and 600 metres (1,300 and 2,000 feet) high. On one of these, Yellow Hill (Huangshan), General Chiang Kai-shek, head of the Guomindang government, built his wartime residence. American, British, French and other allied powers also built ambassadorial residences which are now used as resthouses. On Yu Mountain, another peak, the wife of the legendary founder of the Xia Dynasty (2205–1766 BC), Emperor Dayu, was said to have lived in 2200 BC. Dayu, who gained eternal fame for his diligence in harnessing the rivers of China, was said to have 'passed his house three times and never entered', so dedicated was he to his task.

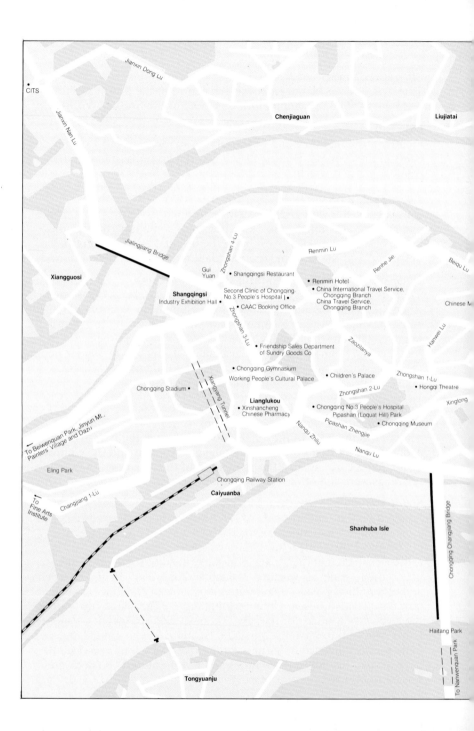

Jianxin Dong Lu

CITS

Chenjiaguan

Liujiatai

Jianxin Nan Lu

Jialingjiang Bridge

Zhongshan 4-Lu

Renmin Lu

Renhe Jie

Beiqu Lu

Xiangguosi

Gui Yuan

• Shangqingsi Restaurant

Shangqingsi
Industry Exhibition Hall •

Second Clinic of Chongqing
No.3 People's Hospital |

• CAAC Booking Office

• Renmin Hotel

• China International Travel Service,
  Chongqing Branch
  China Travel Service,
  Chongqing Branch

Chinese M

Zhongshan 3-Lu

Zaozilanya

Hanwei Lu

• Friendship Sales Department
  of Sundry Goods Co

• Chongqing Gymnasium

Working People's Cultural Palace

• Children's Palace

Zhongshan 1-Lu

Chongqing Stadium •

Xiangyang Tunnel

Lianglukou

Zhongshan 2-Lu

• Hongqi Theatre

Xinglong

• Xinshancheng
  Chinese Pharmacy

• Chongqing No.3 People's Hospital
  Pipashan (Loquat Hill) Park

Nanqu Zhilu

Pipashan Zhengjie

• Chongqing Museum

To Beiwenquan Park, Jinyun Mt.
Painters' Village and Dazu

Nanqu Lu

Eling Park

Chongqing Railway Station

To
Fine Arts
Institute

Changjiang 1-Lu

Caiyuanba

Shanhuba Isle

Chongqing Changjiang Bridge

Haitang Park

To Nanwenquan Park

Tongyuanju

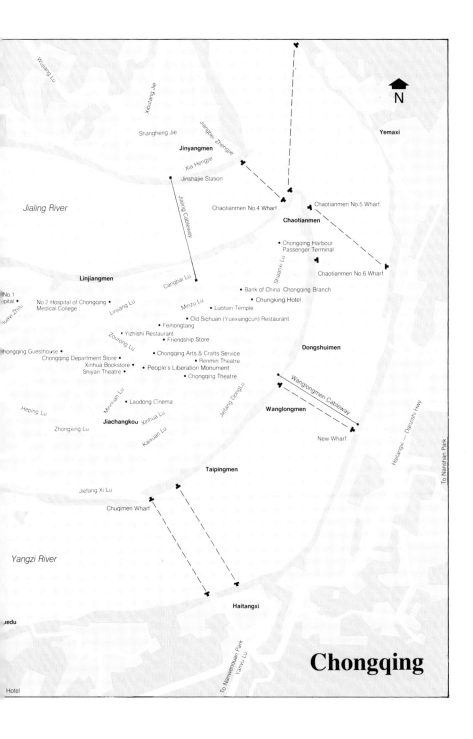

N

Wujiang Lu

Xioutang Jie

Shangheng Jie

Jiangbei Zhengjie

Jinyangmen

Xia Hengjie

Jinshajie Station

*Jialing River*

Jialing Cableway

Yemaxi

Chaotianmen No.4 Wharf

Chaotianmen No.5 Wharf

Chaotianmen

Linjiangmen

Cangbai Lu

• Chongqing Harbour
  Passenger Terminal

Shaanxi Lu

Chaotianmen No.6 Wharf

No.1
spital •

No.2 Hospital of Chongqing •
Medical College

Linjiang Lu

Minzu Lu

• Bank of China  Chongqing Branch

• Chungking Hotel

• Luohan Temple

• Old Sichuan (Yuexiangcun) Restaurant

• Feihongtang

huayi Zhilu

• Yizhishi Restaurant

Zourong Lu

• Friendship Store

Dongshuimen

hongqing Guesthouse •
Chongqing Department Store •
Xinhua Bookstore •
Shiyan Theatre •

• Chongqing Arts & Crafts Service

• Renmin Theatre

• People's Liberation Monument

• Chongqing Theatre

Wanglongmen Cableway

Minmian Lu

• Laodong Cinema

Heping Lu

Jiachangkou

Xinhua Lu

Zhongxing Lu

Kaixuan Lu

Jietang Dong Lu

Wanglongmen

New Wharf

Haitangxi — Danzishi Hwy

To Nanshan Park

Taipingmen

Jietang Xi Lu

Chuqimen Wharf

*Yangzi River*

Haitangxi

uedu

To Nanwenquan Park

Yanyu Lu

# Chongqing

Hotel

## Southern Hot Springs (Nanwen Quan)

These hot springs were first established in the Ming Dynasty (1368–1644), and it was to this spot that the politically disillusioned emperor Jianwen (reigned 1399–1403) retired as a monk. Hot spring baths were first built in the Qing Dynasty (1644–1911) and have been enlarged several times this century. The water temperature remains around 40°C (104°F) all year round. The springs are 26 kilometres (16 miles) south of Chongqing.

## Northern Hot Springs (Beiwen Quan)

The Northern Hot Springs are some 50 kilometres (30 miles) north of Chongqing, by the bank of the Jialing on Wentang Gorge. Historical records reveal that the Warm Spring Temple existed on this site 1,500 years ago, but the present temple dates from the Ming and Qing Dynasties. The four halls rise up the hillside on a central axis. The Guanyin Hall, with iron tiles and stone pillars, is flanked on either side by natural springs. Lotus and fish ponds, ancient trees, bath-houses, restaurants and a guesthouse complete this scenic spot.

A day's visit to the Northern Hot Springs may also include a visit to the **Beipei Natural History Museum** in which fossil remains of three dinosaurs are exhibited.

## Jinyun Mountain

Located near the Northern Hot Springs, the mountain is 1,030 metres (3,380 feet) high and is also known as Little Emei Mountain. Tourists should begin their ascent at Jinyun Temple and climb the 680 steps to Lion's Peak where they may view the nine peaks of Jinyun. The area is a natural botanical garden with 1,700 species of plants and trees.

## Sichuan Fine Arts Institute (Sichuan Meishu Xueyuan)

This is the only residential undergraduate- and graduate-level fine arts college in southwest China, with a student enrolment of around 300 a year. Students come from all over China as well as from abroad. The college was founded in 1950, and has departments of sculpture, painting, crafts (including lacquerware, textile design, packaging design and ceramics) and teacher training. The institute is particularly proud of its gallery, the largest art institute gallery in all China, which displays the best work of its students. The gallery is open to the public 9 am–12 noon and 2.30–5.30 pm. Many of the items are for sale. The institute is located at Huangjiaoping, on the northern bank of the Yangzi, about half an hour's drive from the centre of the city.

## Painters Village (Huajia Zhi Cun)

In pleasant, tranquil surroundings, a group of nationally selected painters and engravers live and work at the Painters Village at

Hualongqiao. This is an interesting place to visit, as much for the works displayed as for a look at how officially recognised artists fare under government patronage. The mostly elderly artists here enjoy what for China are excellent conditions — they have their own studios — and produce an impressive range of work. There is an art gallery within the complex.

## Dazu Buddhist Caves

For tourists staying more than two days in Chongqing, it is possible to make a trip to see the spectacular Buddhist cave carvings of Dazu County. The most comfortable way is obviously to hire a car (upwards of Rmb250 a day) for the excursion. Provided there is no major delay on the busy road, the return journey can be hurriedly done in one day. Otherwise allow for an overnight stay in Dazu and take the bus from Kangfulai Bus Company (tel. 55500) on Renmin Lu, about a ten-minute walk west from the Renmin Guesthouse. The 160-kilometre (100-mile) ride over hilly country can take as long as six hours, but the bus is reasonably comfortable and air-conditioned. At Dazu make for the **Dazu Guesthouse (Dazu Binguan)** at 47 Gongnong Jie (tel. 237), which will provide meals if they are ordered in advance.

Trains leave for Dazu twice a day, taking three hours for the journey.

Forty sites have been discovered, with 50,000 carvings in 290 niches and grottoes. Seven sites are open to the public, but those at Beishan and Baodingshan are the most frequently visited.

The earliest sculptures date from the Tang Dynasty (618−907), when the emperors Xuanzong (reigned 712−56) and Xizong (reigned 873−88) fled to Sichuan as civil war broke out in the north. With them came many monks, painters, sculptors and literati, who transformed Sichuan into a centre of culture. Bas-relief carvings of extraordinary grace and detail continued to be created up to the Ming Dynasty (1368−1644). Figures and stories from the Buddhist pantheon dominate — a giant reclining Buddha, 31 metres (100 feet) long; a statue of Avalokitesvara seated on a lotus flower, her 1,007 hands spread out over 88 square metres (950 square feet) of rock. An unusual feature here is the carving of scenes from everyday life executed with tender vividness.

## Fuling

The river Wu rises in Guizhou and at its confluence with the Yangzi stands the ancient town of Fuling, on the south bank. Some 2,000 years ago Fuling was the political centre of the Kingdom of Ba (fourth to second centuries BC) and the site of its ancestral graves.

Fuling is the connecting link in water transportation between northern Guizhou and eastern Sichuan. The town and its surrounding area are rich in such produce as grain, lacquer and tung oil, and the local specialities are hot pickled mustard tuber, Hundred-Flower sweet wine and pressed radish seeds.

West of the town is the White Crane Ridge, on which are carved ancient water level marks in the form of 14 scaled fish, and many inscriptions referring to the hydrology of the river at this point. These stone fish — the oldest carved in the Tang Dynasty (618–907) — are visible only at lowest water level which occurs perhaps once every decade or so. Locals say that 'when the stone fish appear the harvests will be good.'

In 1972 archaeologists excavated graves from the Kingdom of Ba, and among the finds were ancient musical instruments.

## Fengdu

Fengdu, on the north bank of the river, was in the past more popularly known as the 'City of Ghosts'. There is a temple here dedicated to the

God of Hades. A pilgrim to the temple used to be able to purchase, for the sum of one dollar, a 'Passport to Heaven', stamped by the local magistrate and the abbot. Landmarks in the town bore horrific names — Ghost Torturing Pass, Last Glance at Home Tower, Nothing-to-be-done Bridge. Fengdu's temples display instruments of torture and wild demon images. Shopkeepers kept a basin of water into which customers threw their coins: if they sank they were genuine, but if they floated the coins were ghost money and unacceptable. Boats would moor in mid-stream rather than by the bank in case of attack by ghosts. It seems that the origin of the town's extraordinary reputation dates back to the Han Dynasty (206 BC−AD 220) when two officials, Yin and Wang, became Daoist (Taoist) recluses here and eventually Immortals. When combined, their names mean 'King of the Underworld'.

Today, however, the town is more happily renowned for its tough bamboo mats and lacquerware, as well as for its 'mouldy' beancurd, the local speciality.

## Zhongxian

There are two moving stories about how Zhongxian (Loyal County) got its name. In the Warring States period (475−221 BC), Ba Manzi, a native of Zhongxian, became a general to the army of the Kingdom of Ba. Towards the end of the Chou Dynasty the Kingdom of Ba was in a state of civil war, and Ba Manzi was sent to the Kingdom of Chu to beg military assistance to put down the rebellion. The price demanded by Chu was the forfeit of three Ba cities. Once Chu's troops had helped restore stability to Ba, the King of Chu sent his minister to demand the payoff. Ba Manzi, however, said: 'Though I promised Chu the cities you will take my head in thanks to the King of Chu, for the cities of Ba cannot be given away', whereupon he cut off his own head. Receiving his minister's account, the King of Chu sighed: 'Cities would count as nothing had I loyal ministers like Ba Manzi.' He then ordered that Ba Manzi's head be buried with full honours.

The second tale is of another man of Zhongxian, the valiant general Yan Yan, who served the Minor Han Dynasty (AD 221−63). Captured by the Shu general Zhang Fei, he refused to surrender, saying boldly: 'In my country we had a general who cut off his own head but we do not have a general who surrendered.' Enraged, Zhang Fei ordered Yan's beheading. The doomed general remained perfectly calm as he asked simply, 'Why are you so angry? If you want to cut off my head then give the order, but there is no point in getting angry and upsetting yourself.' Zhang Fei was so deeply moved by Yan's loyalty

and bravery in the face of death that he personally unbound him,
treating him as an honoured soldier.

Traditionally, the thick bamboo hawsers used to haul junks over
the rapids were made in this area, as the local bamboo is especially
tenacious. Today, bamboo handicrafts are a thriving industry, while
the local food speciality is Zhongxian beancurd milk.

## Shibaozhai

Shibaozhai represents the first gem of Chinese architecture to be
encountered on the downstream journey. From afar, the protruding
220-metre (720-foot) high hill on the north bank can appear to
resemble a jade seal, and is so named. The creation of the hill is
attributed to Goddess Nuwo, who caused a rock slide while she was
redecorating the sky after a fierce battle between two warring dukes.

A red pavilion hugs one side of this rock. Its tall yellow entrance
gate is decorated with lions and dragons and etched with an inscription
inviting the visitor to climb the ladder and ascend into a 'Little
Fairyland'. The temple at the top was built during the reign of
Emperor Qianlong (1736–96) and access to it was by an iron chain
attached to the cliff. A nine-storeyed wooden pavilion was added in
1819 so that monks and visitors to the temple would not have to suffer
the discomforts of the chain ascent. In 1956 three more storeys were
added. Each floor is dedicated to famous generals of the Three
Kingdoms period (AD 220–65), local scholars and renowned Chinese
poets.

In front of Ganyu Palace at the top of Jade Seal Hill is the Duck
Hole. It is said that as spring turns to summer, if you take a live duck
and drop it through the hole, it will quickly reappear swimming in the
Yangzi. In the past the monks apparently drew their drinking water
from this hole by using a pipe made of bamboo.

The spirit wall in the temple's main hall is constructed of excavated
Han-Dynasty (206 BC–AD 220) bricks. The hall behind is dedicated
on the right to Generals Zhang Fei and Yan Yan (see above) of the
Three Kingdoms, and on the left to General Qin Liangyu (1576–1648)
who fought bravely against the Manchu forces. A mural shows
Goddess Nuwo repairing the sky. Two side corridors and a back hall
display archaeological finds and portraits of local Qing-Dynasty
officials. Fossils of fish and a tail-section of a dinosaur, found by the
river's edge, can also be seen.

In the rear hall are the remains of the Rice Flowing Hole. Legend
has it that long ago just enough husked rice would flow up from the
small hole each day for the needs of the monks and their guests. One

day a greedy monk, thinking he could become rich, chiselled a bigger hole, and the rice flow ceased forever.

Shibaozhai (population 3,000) is visited from **Xijietou** on the south bank. Disembark here for the local ferries to cross the river.

# Wanxian

About two hours below Shibaozhai the boat reaches Wanxian, which is guarded by two nine-storeyed pagodas for good fortune. The city spreads out on both sides of the river and is known as the Gateway to East Sichuan. It is situated high above the river and the foundations of the buildings are many metres high. Porters vie with each other to carry the passenger's luggage up the steep stairways to the city. The winding streets vary in level from 29 to 206 metres (95 to 675 feet), so bicycles are a rare sight. Wanxian has a number of silk-weaving and spinning factories supported by intense silkworm cultivation — operated on a family basis — which continues year round in Wanxian County. Other light industries include tea, bamboo and cane goods, cotton clothing, leather and Chinese medicines. Paper mills utilizing wheat and rice straw from the countryside disgorge milky waste into the Yangzi, adding to the pollution.

In July 1981 the Yangzi River rose 42 metres (138 feet), flooding much of the lower half of the city for three days.

## *History of Wanxian*

The city received its present name in the Ming Dynasty (1368–1644), and became a foreign Treaty Port in 1902. In 1926 two British gunboats bombarded the city, causing massive fires, when the local warlord took to commandeering foreign vessels for the transport of his troops. Following this incident, a boycott on the loading and unloading of British vessels was enforced for several years. This became known as the Wanxian Incident.

As the halfway city between Yichang and Chongqing, Wanxian was a main port for East Sichuan merchandise (including large quantities of tung oil, used in treating wooden junks). Early travellers commented on the huge number of junks anchored at Wanxian. Junks also used to be built here from cypress wood found in the nearby hills.

## *What to See in Wanxian*

The downriver boats from Chongqing usually reach Wanxian in the early evening, and depart in the small hours of the following morning.

This enables the passage of the Three Gorges to be made in daylight. Upright boats also make a long stop. Passengers rush off the boats, hurrying up the hundreds of steps to the town where every night of the year the famous Wanxian rattan and cane market is held on **Shengli Lu**. Buyers and sellers mingle in a frenzy of bargaining for handmade summer bed mats, fans, hats, straw shoes, furniture and basketry. Small, round, red-trimmed baskets with lids are the most popular item and are well known throughout China. Road-side stalls trade in spicy noodles and cooling, opaque soyabean jelly and fresh fruit.

In the mornings, just a little further west of the night market area, one of the city's ten free markets sells local produce and seasonal delicacies such as mountain mushrooms or live eels. **Second Street (Er Malu)** is the main shopping thoroughfare.

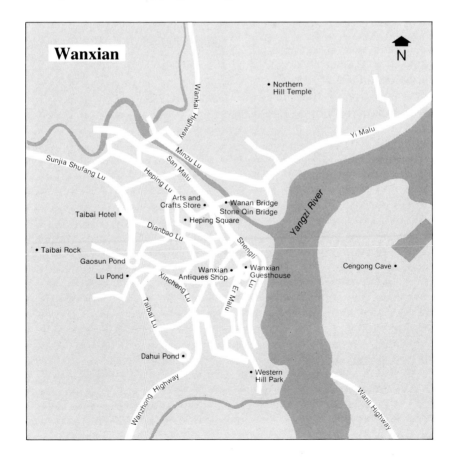

There was a community of foreign missionaries in Sichuan before 1949, and two churches — one Catholic and one Protestant — continue to draw sizeable congregations of country folk.

In 1983 a small workshop was set up, employing two teenage boys and a few part-time workers to paint and varnish river stones from the Three Gorges and from the Daning River's three mini-gorges. These make attractive mementoes and can be bought at the Arts and Crafts Store, 1 Third Street (San Malu).

Visitors may also visit silk-weaving and cane furniture factories.

**Lu Pond and the Xishanpai Pavilion**

This small pool, originally dug by a locally revered Song-Dynasty official, Lu Youkai, was once a very large lotus pond surrounded by decorative pavilions. Now it is not much more than a traffic roundabout. Nearby stands an ancient two-storey, yellow-tiled pavilion which houses a huge rock carved by the calligrapher Huang Tingzhen. Around the Xishanpai Pavilion once flowed a winding freshwater channel. Local literati would spend their evenings here, floating full wine cups along the channel. When a wine cup stopped in front of one of them his forfeit was to compose a poem.

**Western Hill Park**

A clock tower, which dominates the town's skyline from the river, was built in this large park in 1924. The upper part was damaged by Japanese bombs in 1939. There is a memorial to a Russian volunteer pilot whose plane crashed in the river in the same year. During the summer, people relax in bamboo deckchairs under the leafy trees, sipping tea and listening to Sichuan-style opera.

**Stone Qin Bridge**

A natural bridge in the shape of a Chinese zither crosses Chu River which divides the town. It is said that Lu Ban, the patron saint of carpenters, spent a whole night building it.

**Taibai Rock**

The poet Li Bai (701−62) lived here for a time; in the Ming Dynasty a memorial hall was built to commemorate him. Stone inscriptions dating back to the Tang Dynasty are still to be seen.

# Yunyang

The county town of Yunyang (Clouded Sun) is situated on the north bank, 64 kilometres (40 miles) below Wanxian. Opposite, on the south bank, is the handsome Zhang Fei Temple.

The Tang-Dynasty poet, Du Fu (712–70), banished to a minor position in Sichuan, fell ill while travelling through Yunyang and stayed for many months, recuperating and writing poetry.

**Zhang Fei Temple**

Zhang Fei, the 'Tiger General' of the State of Shu during the Three Kingdoms period (AD 220–65), is revered as a man who kept his word. In 221, Guan Yu, Zhang Fei's sworn brother, was killed by the armies of the State of Wu. The Tiger General, then an official in Langzhong County, swore revenge and prepared to attack Wu with his army arrayed in white armour and pennants — white being the colour of mourning. He ordered Commanders Zhang Da and Fan Jiang to lead the attack and avenge his brother, under pain of death. The two pusillanimous officers got Zhang Fei drunk and cut off his head. They then fled by boat to Yunyang, intending to surrender to Wu. Here, however, they heard of a peace settlement between Wu and Shu, and threw Zhang Fei's head into the river, where it circled a fisherman's boat. Zhang Fei appealed to the fisherman in a dream to rescue his head and bury it in Shu. The fisherman obeyed, and the head was interred on Flying Phoenix Hill. A temple was built to commemorate the bold warrior. This is the story behind the ancient saying, 'Zhang Fei's body is buried in Langzhong but his head is in Yunyang.'

It is said that the head was placed in a vat of oil, and when copper cash was thrown into the vat, the head would float up to give advice to the lovelorn and childless.

The temple was partly damaged in the flood of 1870, so most of the present ensemble of buildings dates from the late 19th century. It has been extensively restored in the last few years. Sixty per cent of the temple's rich collections of paintings, tablets and inscriptions were lost during the Cultural Revolution. In front of the main hall are giant statues of the three famous sworn brothers — Liu Bei, Guan Yu and Zhang Fei. Inside the hall sits the wild-eyed, red-faced Zhang Fei; on either side are scenes from his life. The Helpful Wind Pavilion contains steles and huge portraits of the general and his wife. It is said that his spirit, in the form of a helpful wind, frequently assisted passing boats. Junkmen used to stop at the temple to light firecrackers and burn incense in appreciation.

The temple stands amidst tranquil gardens, waterfalls and pools.

# Fengjie

Fengjie stands on the north bank, just above the western entrance to Qutang, the first of the three great Yangzi gorges. Fengjie town, the county seat for the area, has a population of 50,000. It is an attractive town, with part of its Ming-Dynasty city wall intact, including over 100 metres (330 feet) of battlements. The stairways from the ferry pontoons lead up through three old city gates. The town is very lively, thronged with Chinese tourists who have come to visit the famous historical site of Baidi City, nearby. The histories of Fengjie and Baidi City are intertwined.

Tourist boats normally stop here for about 20 minutes, which is long enough to enable ongoing passengers to take a brief stroll about the town. For a visit to Baidi Cheng (see page 58) visitors will have to spend a night at Fengjie. Fengjie's Travel Service (Fengjie Xian Luyouju) is exceptionally helpful.

## *History of Fengjie*

The ancient town was called Kuifu in the Spring and Autumn period (770−476 BC), but became known as Fengjie after the Tang Dynasty (618−907). It has long been famous as a poets' city, as many of China's greatest poets commemorated their visits here with verses. The Tang poet Du Fu (712−70) wrote some 430 poems while serving as an official here for two years.

Liu Bei, the King of Shu during the Three Kingdoms period (AD 220−65), died of despair in the Eternal Peace Palace after he was defeated by the armies of Wu. According to two ancient tablets unearthed in recent years, the Fengjie Teachers Training Institute now stands on the site of the palace. On his deathbed, Liu Bei entrusted his sons to the care of his loyal adviser, Zhuge Liang, entreating him to educate them in wisdom and to choose the most talented one to succeed him as king.

the Eight Battles Diagram (Ba Zhen Tu) where Zhuge Liang trained the troops of Shu in military strategy. The Eight Battle Arrays were in fact 64 one and a half-metre (five-foot) high piles of stones erected in a grid pattern, 24 of which represented the surrounding troops. The principles of Zhuge Liang's manoeuvres have long been studied by China's military strategists and continue to be relevant to present-day concepts of Chinese warfare.

Nearby is the village of Yufu, which means 'the fish turns back' and relates to the legend of Qu Yuan, China's famous poet and statesman of the third century BC. During his service at court, the country was riven by factions and discord. His political enemies had him exiled; eventually, in despair, he drowned himself in Dongting Lake. His body was allegedly swallowed by a sacred fish which then swam up the gorges to Qu Yuan's birthplace, near Zigui (see page 76), where the

fish intended to give Qu Yuan an honourable burial. However, so great were the lamentations and weeping of the mourners along the shore that the fish also became tearful and swam past Zigui. It was not until it reached Yufu that the fish realized its mistake and turned back.

## *What to See in Fengjie*

Fengjie is typical of many of the Yangzi River towns. Its markets on **Zhonghua Lu**, **Heping Lu** and **Fandi Lu** are filled with local produce, clothing and Chinese mountain herbs. Its fruits — especially peaches, pomelos and snow-pears — are famous. Yellow poplar wooden combs were a speciality, but are now rare. **Dadongmen Jie** is lined with leafy trees and traditional whitewashed two-storeyed houses — the upper storey frequently in wood — and was once called Zhuge Liang Jie, for it is said he passed this way. Outside the city wall, above the river, are makeshift matshed teahouses where the local men and travellers relax in bamboo deckchairs, drinking tea and eating sunflower seeds or eggs boiled in tea; others smoke their pipes, chatting with friends or playing mahjong or cards. When summer floods threaten, these temporary sheds are simply dismantled and re-erected once the water subsides.

## Baidi Cheng (White Emperor City)

The local ferry from Fengjie takes about 20 minutes to reach Baidi Cheng on the north bank of the river, passing several pagodas on the surrounding peaks (the return trip takes an hour). Sadly the approach to this historic site is quite spoilt by a factory and workers' housing built in the 1970s.

Because of its strategic position the town was chosen in the first century by Gong Sunshu, an official turned soldier, as the site of his headquarters. The legend goes that in AD 25 white vapour in the shape of a dragon was seen rising from a nearby well. Taking this as an auspicious omen, Gong declared himself the 'White Emperor' and the town 'White Emperor City'. Remains of the city wall can still be seen on the hill behind Baidi Mountain. The 12-year reign of the White Emperor was regarded as a time of peace and harmony, so after his death a temple was built to commemorate his reign. This temple dates back over 1,950 years.

Several hundred steps lead up the wooded Baidi Mountain. The **Western Pavilion** (at one time known as Guanyin Dong) on the slope is believed to have been occupied by the great poet Du Fu, who wrote numerous poems at this site. The pavilion overlooks what Du Fu described as 'the limitless Yangzi'. Further up the hill is a stupa, marking the grave of a much-loved literary monk who served at the temple during the Qing Dynasty.

A red wall with an imposing yellow dragonhead gateway surrounds the temple complex. Though the temple was originally dedicated to Gong Sunshu, the White Emperor, his statue was removed in the Ming Dynasty (1368–1644) and replaced with images of Liu Bei, Zhuge Liang, Guan Yu and Zhang Fei, heroes of the Shu Kingdom during the Three Kingdoms period. The present halls date from the Ming Dynasty.

The front hall contains large modern statues which depict Liu Bei on his deathbed entrusting his sons to the care of Zhuge Liang (see page 55). To the left is the handsome, winged **Observing the Stars Pavilion (Guanxing Ting)**, where a large bronze bell can be seen hanging in the upper storey. From this pavilion Zhuge Liang observed the stars and made accurate weather forecasts which helped him plan his victorious battles. The two **Forest of Tablets** halls contain several rare engraved steles, some over 1,300 years old. The Phoenix Tablet is particularly finely engraved. The Bamboo Leaf Poem Tablet is one of only three in China. It is considered a fine work of art, combining as it does poetry and calligraphy, for the tablet is engraved with three branches of bamboo, each leaf forming the Chinese characters of a poem.

The **Wuhou Hall** is dedicated to Zhuge Liang, his son and grandson. The bodies of the statues are of the Ming Dynasty, but the heads, smashed in the Cultural Revolution, are new. **Mingliang Hall** is dedicated to Liu Bei, who is shown surrounded by four attendants, as well as the black-faced Zhang Fei and the red-faced Guan Yu on one side, and Zhuge Liang on the other. Adjoining rooms display furniture, scrolls, porcelain and other cultural relics.

In 1987, several buildings were converted to form a museum displaying the many cultural relics found within the area, including two coffins from the Ba culture. One of these dates back to the Western Han Dynasty.

Fine views of the entrance to Qutang Gorge can be seen from the temple. If the proposed Three Gorges Dam is built further downriver in the Xiling Gorge, near Yichang, the water level will rise and Baidi Mountain will become an island.

At the foot of Baidi Mountain, the Yanyu Rock — over 30 metres (100 feet) long, 20 metres (66 feet) wide and 40 metres (130 feet) high — used to be a constant hazard to boats riding the swift current and heading into the narrow entrance of Qutang Gorge. Over the ages, countless vessels perished. In 1959 it took a work team seven days to blow up this gigantic rock.

## Qutang Gorge

Immediately below Baidi City is **Kui Men**, the entrance to the first of the three gorges of the Yangzi River — the eight-kilometre (five-mile) long Qutang Gorge (also known by early Western travellers as the Wind Box Gorge). The shortest but grandest of them all, the gorge's widest point is only 150 metres (500 feet). Mists frequently swirl around the mysterious limestone peaks, some nearly 1,200 metres (4,000 feet) high, and the river rushes swift as an arrow through the narrow entrance, pounding the perpendicular cliff faces of the gorge.

This gorge was a particularly dangerous stretch during high water levels and has been known to rise to 146 metres (480 feet). An upper Yangzi steamboat captain recalled how in September 1929 the level of water was 75 metres (246 feet), and likened the passage to a trough, with the water banked up on both sides. His ship became quite unmanageable, and was carried down, broadside on, only coming under control again at the lower end. He would never, he vowed, try to negotiate it again at such a level.

Two mountains — the **Red Passage Mountain (Chijia Shan)** to the north, once compared to a celestial peach, and the **White Salt Mountain (Baiyan Shan)** to the south — form the Kui Men entrance, their steep precipices like the wings of a giant door guarding the tumultuous waters.

In the Tang Dynasty (618–907) chains were strung across the river as an 'iron lock' to prevent passage of enemy boats. In the Song Dynasty (960–1279) two iron pillars nearly two metres (six feet) tall were erected on the north side and seven chains, some 250 metres (820 feet) long, were used to block the river passage. Although the original purpose was defensive, the chain-locks were later used to enable local authorities to gather taxes from all boats travelling downriver. This system continued until the middle Qing Dynasty. The iron pillars are only visible at low water.

On the precipice of White Salt Mountain (south side) are a series of holes nearly a metre (three feet) apart and about a third of a metre (one foot) deep, forming a 'Z' shape. These are known as the **Meng Liang Stairway**. According to legend, Yang Jiye, a Song-Dynasty general, was buried on a terrace high up on the mountain. His loyal comrade-in-arms, Meng Liang, decided secretly to take the bones back for burial in Yang's home town. In the dead of night he took a small boat into the gorge and began to hack out a pathway to the terrace. Halfway up the rock face he was discovered by a monk who began crowing like a cock. Meng Liang, thinking that dawn was breaking and fearing discovery, abandoned his task. When he later discovered the

monk's mischief, he was so provoked that he hung the monk upside down over a precipice. The rock below Meng Liang Stairway is known as **Hanging Monk Rock (Daodiao Heshangshi)**. History records, however, that General Yang was not buried here and the steps are probably the remains of an ancient river pathway. Sections of a city wall, 1,400 years old, have been found on top of White Salt Mountain, so it is possible that the pathway led to this early settlement. Another theory about the stairway suggests that it was built to provide access to the rare medicinal herbs which grow high on the cliff faces.

At the highest point above Hanging Monk Rock one can see **Armour Cave (Kuangjia Dong)** where it is said a Song-Dynasty woman general hid her arms. In 1958 the cave was explored and found to contain three 2,000-year old wooden coffins from the Kingdom of Ba, in which were bronze swords and lacquered wooden combs.

Near the Meng Liang Stairway is the **Drinking Phoenix Spring**, a stalagmite in the shape of a phoenix drinking the sweet spring-water. Nearby is the **Chalk Wall (Fengbi Tang)** where 900 characters, dating from the Song Dynasty, have been carved by famous calligraphers on the rock face. The site derives its name from the limestone powder which was used to smooth rock surfaces before being carved.

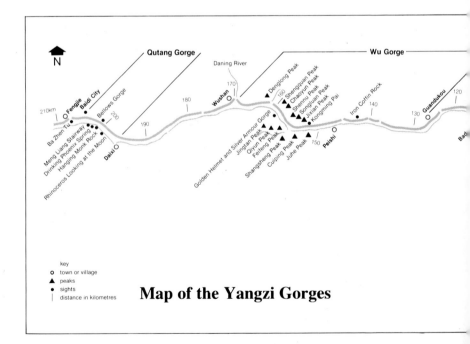

**Map of the Yangzi Gorges**

On the north side of the river, opposite Meng Liang Stairway, is a coffee-coloured precipice called **Bellows Gorge (Fengxiang Xia)**. The name refers to some square configurations in the rock face, which were supposed to be bellows used by Lu Ban, the God of Carpenters. In 1971 the secret of Bellows Gorge was revealed, when ancient suspended wooden coffins, similar to those found in the Armour Cave, were discovered in the caves of the precipice. Some of these have been moved to museums, but three remain and can be seen from the river.

**Wise Grandmother's Spring (Shenglao Quan)** in a rock crevice on the southern bank was, according to legend, created by an immortal grandmother from heaven for thirsty travellers. They had only to call out to the spring 'Worthy Grandmother, a drink!' and water would gush for a moment from the rock. When the call was repeated, water would again spurt forth.

East of Armour Cave (on the south side), on the top of a black rock, is a huge stone which the Chinese say resembles the body of a rhinoceros looking westwards as if forever enjoying 'the autumn moon over the gorge gate'. They call this rock **Rhinoceros Looking at the Moon**.

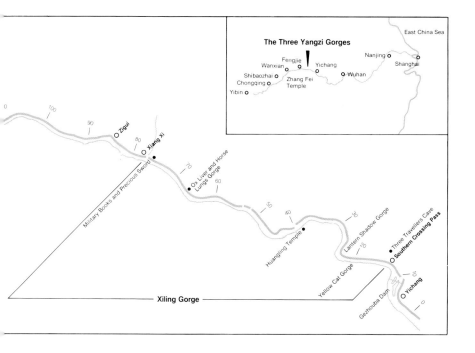

From Baidi City to Wushan through the whole length of Qutang Gorge, visitors may see, high up on the northern face, the old towpath, hand-hewn in 1889 by the local people. Prior to this there existed a smaller towpath which was often submerged at high water. Remnants of this path can still be seen below Bellows Gorge. Travellers had to abandon their boats and climb over the peaks, a dangerous and time-wasting detour. Boats going upstream had to wait for a favourable east wind; if the wind was in the wrong quarter, boats would be stranded in the water for ten days or more.

The sandstone walls of the gorges have become pitted by natural erosion, causing lines of holes, some of which are several metres deep.

The town of **Daixi**, at the mouth of a stream bearing the same name, marks the eastern end of Qutang Gorge. Over 200 burial sites have been found here, and excavations have revealed a rich collection of bone, stone and jade artifacts and pottery, as well as various burial forms of the middle and late New Stone Age period.

Below Daixi the river widens out. About five kilometres (three miles) downstream, on the south bank, are two sharp, black peaks which form the **Unlocked Gates Gorge (Suokai Xia)**. On the west side of the gorge, mid-way up the mountain, is a semi-circular stone shaped roughly like a drum — this is the **Beheading Dragon Platform (Zhanglong Tai)**. Facing this on the opposite side of the gorge is a thick, round stone pillar — the **Binding Dragon Pillar (Suolong Zhu)**. Once upon a time, the Jade Dragon, a son of the Dragon of the Eastern Sea, lived in a cave on the upper reaches of the Daixi Stream. One season he decided to visit his family by way of the Yangzi, but shortly afterwards found himself lost. Changing into the form of an old man, he asked his way of a herdsboy. The boy pointed north with his sickle. The dragon rushed off in that direction but again got lost, whereupon he flew into a mighty rage and rushed at the mountains, causing them to crumble and dam up the river; farmlands were flooded, earthquakes toppled houses, and men and animals perished. At this moment the Goddess Yao Ji rushed to the spot on an auspicious cloud. She rebuked Jade Dragon, but he was unrepentant. She flung a string of pearls into the air; it changed into a rope that bound the dragon to the stone pillar. Yao Ji then ordered the great Da Yu, Controller of Rivers, to behead the murderous dragon on the nearby platform. He then diverted the river by cutting the gorge. The people of this valley have lived happily ever since.

Two kilometres (1.2 miles) further on, the Baozi Tan (a triple rapid) and the Xiama Tan used to be serious dangers to shipping at low-water level. A traveller on one of the Yangzi steamships in the 1930s remarked:

Only the throbbing of the engines as the bow entered the most turbulent part
of the rapid, and buried its nose deep in the boiling water, revealed its
presence to the uninitiated. But on looking back one could see that there had
been a drop of two or three feet in the water where the rapid was most violent.
Above it was a series of whirlpools and races.

## Wushan

Wushan County is situated above the Yangzi on the north bank and
embraced by lovely mountain peaks where flourishes the tung tree,
whose oil was used for the caulking, oiling and varnishing of junks and
sampans. The small town of Wuxia, with 15,000 residents, is the
county seat. Wuxia is the starting point for boat trips up the beautiful
Daning River — the main reason for making a stop at Wushan.

### *History of Wushan*

The town has existed since the latter part of the Shang Dynasty
(*c.*1600−1027 BC). In the Warring States period (475−221 BC) the
King of Chu established a palace west of the city. During the first
century the faith of the Buddha had reached China and many temples
were built here; almost all the temples have been destroyed over the
years. The name of the town originates with Wu Xian, a successful
Tang-Dynasty doctor to the imperial court, who was buried on Nanling
Mountain, on the south bank opposite Wushan. A winding path —
with 108 bends — leads from the foot of the mountain to the summit
where there is a small temple. This path was an official road through to
Hubei Province in ancient times.

### *What to See in Wushan*

The streets of this long and narrow town are named after the 12 peaks
of the Wu Gorge. The old houses are mostly two-storeyed, with central
courtyards on whose walls hang baskets of dried medicinal herbs. The
markets supply the essentials for mountain living — back-baskets,
broad-brimmed woven hats with plastic or waxed paper crowns to keep
off the frequent summer rains, plastic and straw sandals (best for
coping with the slippery mud after rain) and agricultural tools. Several
street dentists with pedal-driven drills await customers. Some
householders still use traditional stone grinders and pounders to make
their wheat and rice flour. There is a fine old Chinese medicine shop at
38 Songluan Jie.

Although there is little left of the many temples here, one may
visit, weather permitting, Gaoqiu Mountain, to the northwest of the

town. This was the site of the King of Chu's palace and of Gaotang
Temple, built to commemorate the Fairy Goddess Yao Ji and Emperor
Da Yu, Controller of Rivers. According to the Daoist (Taoist) legend,
it was on this site that Da Yu camped while cutting the three Yangzi
River Gorges.

At the top of this mountain is the village of Zhaojun. The name
commemorates a Han-Dynasty heroine whose father was born here.
The beautiful Wang Zhaojun was a maid of honour to the imperial
court. At that time, court procedure required portraits to be painted of
each maid of honour, the most beautiful of whom were chosen by the
emperor for his concubines. Court painters became rich on the bribes
they received from these aspiring ladies. Zhaojun, however, refused to
bribe the artist, and in revenge, he painted her as an ugly woman.
Zhaojun was to spend a lonely and bitter time in the palace before
being noticed by the emperor, who immediately became enamoured of
her (see page 77). Since Zhaojun came to the village often as a child, a
stone tablet was erected in her memory, and the custom arose of
unmarried girls coming here and burning their foreheads, disfiguring
and therefore disqualifying themselves from court service.

The energetic visitor may climb to the summit of Wushan (Witches
Hill), a two-hour hike. Worshippers still come to a small shrine here,
built within the ruins of an old Buddhist monastery. From the summit
the views of Wu Gorge and the river are spectacular. A less strenuous
outing may be made to the newly opened limestone cave complex in

Wu Gorge high up on the cliff face above the south bank of the river. This involves a short boat ride from Wushan town, an easy scramble up the rocky slope and then a walk along the old towpath. Around the cave complex there are the usual teahouse and ornamental pavilions. The cave complex, Luyou Dong, is named after a Song-Dynasty official who visited Wushan and left an appreciative record of his stay.

**Daning River Excursion**
This breathtakingly beautiful area has been opened to foreign tourism only since 1985 and for this reason it remains unspoilt. A day trip up the crystal-clear Daning River through its magnificent three mini-gorges (Xiao Sanxia) — whose total length is only 33 kilometres (20 miles) — is to experience the excitement and awe of bygone days of river travel in China.

The excursion is undertaken in long, low wooden motorized sampans, whose strong experienced boatmen pole with all their might when the river is too shallow for the engine to be used, heaving their bodies forward as they thrust long iron-tipped bamboo poles into the riverbed, and following through until they are almost lying on their backs in their struggle against the current. Few of the local boats encountered are motorized and the boatmen must tow the boats — laden with local merchandise and coal — upriver, using a long bamboo rope and tracking in harness, along the water's edge or along cut pathways in the rock face, chanting as they go. To negotiate a rapid may take several exhausting attempts before the boat is hauled over.

About 40 minutes from the mouth of the river, at its confluence with the Yangzi, the entrance to the first of the gorges is reached. This is the **Dragon Door Gorge (Longmen Xia)**, three kilometres (1.8 miles) long. On the cliff face to the right is the 1981 flood mark, over 40 metres (130 feet) above river level. The mouth of the gorge is like a massive gateway through which the river rushes like a green dragon, hence its name. The gateway appears to shut once one has passed through. On the east side is **Dragon Door Spring (Longmen Quan)** and above it **Lingzhi Peak**, topped by the **Nine-Dragon Pillar**. On this peak, it is said, grow strange plants and flowers and the fungus of longevity (*lingzhi*), guarded by nine dragons. On the western bank, two rows of 15-centimetre (two-inch) square holes which continue the entire length of the small gorges and number over 6,000 are all that remain of an astonishing plank walkway first constructed in the Han period and recorded in the Annals of Wushan County in 246 BC. Wooden stakes inserted into these hand-hewn holes supported planks and large bamboo pipes, which stretched for 100 kilometres (62 miles) along the river. The pipeline conveyed brine, while the planks provided a maintenance and access way. In the 17th century the pathway, used by the peasant leader Li Zicheng in his uprising against the Ming Dynasty, was destroyed by the imperial army.

After leaving the gorge the boat passes the **Nest of Silver Rapid (Yinwo Tan)**. In the past, rich merchants trading in the hinterland often came to grief here; perhaps there are caches of silver under the bubbling surface still! In 1958 work began on clearing major obstacles from the river.

The Daning then meanders through terraced hillsides before entering the ten-kilometre (six-mile) **Bawu Gorge**, with its dramatic scenery of rocks, peaks and caves (among them, Fairy Maiden Cave, Fairy Throwing a Silk Ball, and Guanyin Seated on a Lotus Platform). A long layered formation, like a scaly dragon, can be seen on the eastern cliff. Suspended upon the precipice is a relic of the ancient inhabitants of eastern Sichuan, the 'iron' coffin (which is actually made of wood that has turned black with age). This gorge is accordingly also known as Iron Coffin Gorge.

The village of **Twin Dragons** or **Shuanglong** (population 300), above Bawu Gorge, is the halfway point. Lunch is provided at the reception centre, which also has ten rooms for overnight accommodation.

**Vivid Green Gorge (Dicui Xia)**, 20 kilometres (12.5 miles) long, is inhabited by wild ducks and covered with luxuriant bamboo groves from which rises a deafening cacophany of birdsong. The famous Golden Monkeys of Sichuan can still be seen if you are lucky. Once their shrill cries resounded throughout the Yangzi gorges, but today they can be heard only in Dicui Gorge. River stones of an extraordinary variety and colour can be gathered. These are painted and sold as artistic souvenirs in Wanxian (see page 50).

At the end of this gorge the tourist boat turns around and rushes downstream, arriving at Wushan in half the time, aided by the skilful use of the long *yuloh*, which is weighted by a stone to steady the boat.

Groups may hire a boat for this trip at approximately Rmb160. Cheap local ferries also do this trip but it takes much longer and requires an overnight stop at Dachang (a town with fine farmhouse architecture and the remains of a Qing-Dynasty city gate); to do this you are required to be accompanied by an official from Wushan.

## Wu Xia (Witches Gorge)

Below Wushan the river approaches the entrance to the 40-kilometre (25-mile) long Wu Gorge, the middle Yangzi gorge which straddles Sichuan and Hubei Provinces. So sheer are the cliffs that it is said the sun rarely penetrates. The boat passes, on the south side, the **Golden Helmet and Silver Armour Gorge (Jinkuang Yinjia Xia)** shaped, it is said, like an ancient warrior's silver coat of arms crowned by a round

golden helmet. Ahead are the 12 peaks of Wu Gorge, famed for their dark and sombre grace. Poets have attempted to evoke both their bleakness and beauty.

*Autumn Thoughts*
Jade dews deeply wilt and wound the maple woods;
On Witch Mountain, in Witch Gorge, the air is sombre, desolate.
Billowy waves from the river roar and rush towards the sky
Over the frontier pass, wind and clouds sink to the darkening earth.
These clustered chrysanthemums, twice blooming, evoke the tears of yesteryear;
A lonely boat, as ever, is moored to the heart that yearns for home.
To cut winter clothes, women everywhere ply their scissors and foot-rulers —
Below the White Emperor's tall city is heard the urgent pounding of the evening wash.

Six peaks line the north side:
Climbing Dragon Peak (Denglong Feng)
Sage Spring Peak (Shengquan Feng)
Facing Clouds Peak (Chaoyun Feng)
Goddess Peak (Shennu Feng)
Fir Tree Cone Peak (Songluan Feng)
Congregated Immortals Peak (Jixian Feng)
Three peaks flank the south side:
Assembled Cranes Peak (Juhe Feng)
Misty Screen Peak (Cuiping Feng)
Flying Phoenix Peak (Feifeng Feng)
and three more may be glimpsed behind these:
Clean Altar Peak (Jingtan Feng)
Rising Cloud Peak (Qiyun Feng)
Mounting Aloft Peak (Shangsheng Feng)
More often than not these green-clad peaks are hidden by swirls of cloud and mist, and are difficult to distinguish though each has its own characteristics and posture.

The most famous is the **Shennu Peak (Goddess Peak)** — also referred to as Observing the Clouds Peak — which resembles the figure of a maiden kneeling in front of a pillar. She is believed to be the embodiment of Yao Ji, the 23rd daughter of the Queen Mother of the West. Yao Ji, at the age of 18, was sent to oversee the Jade Pool of the Western Heaven, accompanied by 11 fairy handmaidens. But she found life there lonely and cold, and took to rambling among the mountains and rivers of the mortal world. Wushan became her favourite place, and there she established a small palace. Once, returning from a visit to the Eastern Sea on her floating cloud, she came upon 12 dragons playing havoc with the river and the mountains, and causing flooding and hardship in their wake. She summoned Da

Yu the Great from his work on the Yellow River and, alighting from her cloud, presented him with a heavenly supernatural book. This endowed him with powers to call upon the wind, rain, thunder and lightning to move the earth, thus enabling his sacred ox to slash open the gorges (ever since all oxen have had bent horns), and permit the waters to drain into the Eastern Sea.

Yao Ji resolved to stay here with her 11 maidens to protect the boats from the dangerous rapids, the peasants' crops from damage, the woodcutters from wild animals, and to grow the fungus of longevity for the sick. Eventually these 12 maidens became the 12 sentinel peaks of Wu Gorge. There are, of course, many variations to this story.

As the river twists and turns, a mountain appears as if to block the way. This is **Congregated Immortals Peak**, on whose greyish-white rock face can just be made out a carved inscription, known as the **Kongming Pai**, which legend attributed to the great third-century politician and strategist Zhuge Liang. However, it seems that the inscription was in fact carved during the Ming Dynasty by the local people to show their eternal respect and regard for this hero.

Five kilometres (three miles) below Kongming Pai on the south bank is the small trading town of **Peishi**, which marks the provincial border between Sichuan and Hubei. Guo Morou, a 20th-century poet, wrote that at this point 'the prow of one's boat is already in Hubei while the stern is still in Sichuan.'

Whitewashed villages cling to the mountain terraces which produce grain crops and fruits — apples, persimmons, peaches, apricots and Chinese chestnuts.

Further along, on the north bank, is the **Iron Coffin Rock (Tieguan Feng)**. If you look carefully you may be able to discern the shape of a yellow coffin and the outline of a figure kneeling in front of it. It is believed that this was a son weeping for his mother. Heaven was so moved by his filial piety that he was turned to stone and remembered by all mankind thereafter.

Just above the north-bank town of **Guandukou** — marking the end of Wu Gorge — was the Flint Rapid (Huoyan Shi), which was very violent at high water. Limestone rocks jutted into the river like huge stone gates beckoning helpless craft. These, along with all the dangerous rocks in the shipping channel, were blown up in the 1950s. Besides rapids, other dangers to navigators included whirlpools, quicksand and currents which varied from hour to hour.

## Badong

Badong, the county seat, has developed around one main street, extending from a power station at the eastern end to factories spreading along three or four hill slopes to the west. It is the

westernmost county town of Hubei Province. Labourers, pitch black from coal-dust, with staff in hand, negotiate the steep slopes above the river, humping back-baskets of coal as they load and unload river lighters. Houses with wooden balconies huddle together on pillars embedded in solid concrete foundations above the bank of the river.

In ancient times, Badong was situated on the other side of the Yangzi and belonged to the State of Ba; in the Song Dynasty (960–1279) the town was moved to the southern bank.

Badong has two pavilions of architectural interest — the **Autumn Wind Pavilion (Qiufeng Ting)** and the **White Cloud Pavilion (Beiyun Ting)**. Local products include tung oil, lacquer, tea, medicinal herbs and animal skins.

## Zigui

Qu Yuan, one of China's greatly loved patriotic poets, was born in 340 BC in the Qu family village very near Zigui. The fame of the present-day walled town, on the north bank, dates from this period long ago.

Qu Yuan's Memorial Hall, with its distinctive white gateway and walls edged in red, is visible on the hillside east of the town. It contains a Ming-Dynasty statue of the poet, as well as stone inscriptions.

The great poet served as a chancellor to King Huai of the Kingdom of Chu, with special responsibility for the royal clans. The king had complete trust in him until discord developed amongst the clans and Qu was falsely slandered. Banished from the capital, he wandered about in Hubei Province, deeply sad and bitter. His poetry and essays reveal his romanticism, loyalty and patriotism. Qu had vigorously advocated that the State of Chu stand firm against attack by the Qin state, but his advice had gone unheeded, and in May of the year 278 BC, he drowned himself in Dongting Lake at the age of 62.

According to historical records, the local people scoured Dongting Lake for his body, beating drums and racing their boats in the course of their search. This event came to be commemorated each May, and to this day the Dragon Boat Festival (Duanwu Jie) is held in the river towns up and down the Yangzi and in many other parts of China. *Zongzi* — sweetened rice steamed in leaves and tied with reeds — was thrown into the water as a sacrifice to Qu Yuan. The tradition of eating *zongzi* at this festival continues, even in Beijing.

There are many fairy tales about Qu Yuan. East of Zigui is a bay named after him. It is said that when he died, a huge fish swallowed him up and swam all the way from Dongting Lake past Zigui to Yufu and back again, where it disgorged the body, amazingly still intact (see also page 55). In his home village is the Qu Field which he allegedly tilled. It is said that he never forgot his ancestral home; to the farmers there he introduced a jade-white rice which was soft and fragrant. Locals remember him at each new rice harvest.

## Xiang Xi (Fragrant Stream)

A small stream just below Zigui and above the entrance to Xiling Gorge is well known to all Chinese as the home of the beautiful Han-Dynasty (206 BC–AD 220) heroine Wang Zhaojun (see also page 67). Her story is the quintessence of virtuous patriotism.

Zhaojun, a maid of honour to the emperor, refused to bribe the painter from whose portraits of the court ladies the emperor traditionally chose his concubines. In revenge, the painter portrayed her as being quite hideous, and so imperial favour was denied her. In 22 BC the emperor, wishing to make a marriage alliance with the northern Xiongnu king, hit upon Wang Zhaojun. Only then did he set eyes on her; he was captivated but it was too late. Married to the Xiongnu king, Zhaojun was able to exert a good influence on relations between the Xiongnu and Han peoples, which gained her great respect. The emperor, in his rage at having lost her, decreed the beheading of the corrupt court painter.

Local people say that before her marriage, Wang Zhaojun returned to her home town and, when washing in the stream, dropped a precious pearl which caused the stream to become crystal-clear and fragrant.

## Xiling Gorge

Xiling Gorge starts at Xiang Xi and zigzags for 76 kilometres (47 miles) down to Yichang. It is the longest and historically the most dangerous of the Yangzi gorges. Before the passage was made safe in the 1950s, 'the whole surface of the water was a swirling mass of whirlpools sucking the froth they created into their centres.' Xiling comprises seven small gorges and two of the fiercest rapids in the stretch of the Yangzi between Chongqing and Yichang.

On entering the western entrance the boat passes through the four-kilometre (2.4-mile) long **Military Books and Precious Sword Gorge (Bingshu Baojian Xia)**. The name of the gorge refers to a stratified layer of rock resembling a stack of books, and a perpendicular rock shaft below it, at a small cave on the north bank. There are two stories told of these formations, both concerning heroes from the classical novel *Romance of the Three Kingdoms*. One legend has it that Zhuge Liang (181–234), military adviser to the King of Shu, became seriously ill while passing this way. Unwilling to entrust his valuable military treatises to any member of his entourage, he placed them up here on this inaccessible ledge, to be kept safe for later

generations. The second tale is about General Zhang Liang of the Kingdom of Shu. It was he who devised the stratagems which enabled Liu Bei, the king, to defeat the Kingdom of Chu and establish the Minor Han Dynasty (AD 221−63). Afraid that he would eventually fall out of favour, Zhang Liang retired from official life and went into seclusion, hiding his military writings and sword here.

A large cleft rock stands at the mouth of a ravine — **Rice Granary Gorge (Micang Xia)** — on the south side. Fine sand, blown by river winds, piles up on this rock, and slowly sifts through a hole underneath. People call this Zhuge Liang's Granary.

Further on, the perilous **Xin Tan** or **New Rapid** rushes over submerged rocks, the oily surface of the water churned up by whirlpools. In 1524, rock slides from the northern mountainside created this 3.2-kilometre (1.9-mile) long, triple-headed rapid. The fall of the riverbed had been estimated at about six metres (20 feet), but today it has a drop of only two metres (6.5 feet). When the water level was low, junks would unload their cargo and be hauled over by 100 or more trackers. Passengers would join their boat beyond the rapid after walking along a winding mountain track and passing through the village of Xintan, once the site of the White Bone Pagoda — a giant pile of bleached bones, which was all that survived of the many thousands who had lost their lives at this frightening place. In 1941 the steamboat *Minxi* came to grief and several hundred people perished. The swift current carried boats downriver through Xin Tan at the rate of seven metres (30 feet) per second.

In 1854 a local merchant collected subscriptions from river traders and built three life-saving craft to patrol this rapid, and to salvage boats and survivors. This was the beginning of the Yangzi River Lifeboat Office, which eventually maintained its red boats on all the danger spots along the Chongqing−Yichang stretch until the 1940s.

The channel winds east and then southwards, towards **Ox Liver and Horse Lungs Gorge**, apparently named after the yellow stalactite formations on the north side. One of the 'Horse's Lungs' is missing, blown up by British gunboats during the reign of Guangxu (1875−1908).

In the middle stretch of Xiling Gorge, the strangely lovely **Kongling Gorge** towers above the iron-green rocks of the 2.5-kilometre (1.5-mile) long **Kongling Tan**, the worst of all the Yangzi rapids. Seventeen catastrophes involving steamships occurred here between 1900 and 1945. The larger boulders choking the channel had names such as 'Big Pearl', 'Monk's Rock' and 'Chickens' Wings', but the deadliest of all was known as 'Come to Me'.

As the boat enters **Yellow Ox Gorge (Huangniu Xia)** — said to look like a man riding an ox — the passage widens out and sweeps under

the ancient **Huangling Temple (Huangling Miao)** on the south face,
nestling amidst orange and pomelo trees. The great poet Du Fu wrote
of his journey through this gorge:

Three dawns shine upon the Yellow Ox.
Three sunsets — and we go so slowly.
Three dawns — again three sunsets —
And we do not notice that our hair is white as silk.

Huangling Temple, said to have been first built during the Spring
and Autumn period (770−476 BC), is dedicated to the great Da Yu
who, with his yellow ox, controlled the flood waters and dug the gorges
(see page 72). The present hall was built in the Ming Dynasty
(1368−1644) and houses a statue of Da Yu, as well as stone
inscriptions. Zhuge Liang is also said to have dug the Yellow Ox
Spring (or Toad Rock, as it is sometimes called) nearby. Its clear
water, according to the Tang-Dynasty *Book of Teas*, was excellent for
the brewing of tea, and Yellow Ox was classified as the Fourth Spring
under Heaven.

After passing below Huangling Temple, the **Bright Moon Gorge
(Mingyue Xia)** and the **Lantern Shadow Gorge (Dengying Xia)** loom
ahead. The latter is overlooked on the south side in the shape
of four figures from *Pilgrimage to the West* (also known as *Monkey*).
This novel is loosely based on the travels of the monk Xuan Zang, who
undertook a perilous journey to India in search of Buddhist scriptures
to take back to China. The tales about his amazing companions and
their escapades have been much loved by generations of Chinese.
When the evening sun's rays fall upon these peaks, the figures do
appear life-like — Xuan Zang standing on the precipice edge; Monkey
(Sun Wukong) peering into the distance; Sandy (Sha Heshang)
carrying the luggage; and Pigsy (Zhu Bajie) riding a horse, all
silhouetted against the fading light like characters in a shadow play.

The last of the smaller gorges is **Yellow Cat Gorge (Huangmao Xia)**,
so named from the yellow cat-shaped rock on the riverside. 'Qi
Taigong Fishing' is the name given to a rock beside a cave on the south
face, because of its fancied resemblance to a bearded old man wearing
yellow trousers.

Now the boat reaches the strategic **Southern Crossing Pass (Nanjin
Guan)**, with Three Travellers' Cave above (see page 85), marking the
end of Xiling Gorge and the three great Yangzi gorges. The river
widens dramatically and ahead lies Gezhouba Dam and Yichang.

## Gezhouba Dam

The massive 70-metre (230-foot) high Gezhouba Dam arrests the
Yangzi's flow and forces all shipping up and down the gorges to pass

through one of its three shiplocks. The dam is the largest in China and the first stage — begun in 1970 — was completed in 1981; the second stage, due for completion in 1988 or 1989, will have an estimated hydroelectric production capacity of 14 billion kilowatt hours per annum. The dam consists of locks, silt-prevention dikes, silt-clearing sluices, spillways and power plants. Visits to the dam are arranged at Yichang.

## Yichang

Situated at the eastern mouth of the gorges, Yichang is the administrative centre of nine surrounding counties. Its population of 420,000 is engaged in light industry, chemical and steel production as well as construction of the Gezhouba Dam.

### *History of Yichang*

History records that as early as 278 BC the town was razed to the ground in a battle between the armies of Chu and Qin. In the Three Kingdoms period 50,000 Wu troops set fire to the encampments of the Shu army, utterly routing Liu Bei, who retreated upriver to Baidi Cheng (see page 58).

Yichang was the transshipment point for cargoes up and down the river. Here, cargoes were unloaded from the larger boats plying the stretch of river between Yichang and Wuhan, and reloaded on to smaller ones running between Yichang and Chongqing. An American traveller in 1921 described the port as 'crowded, incessantly busy, a perfect maelstrom of sampans, junks, lighters with cargo, steamers and gunboats.' It was declared a foreign Treaty Port in 1876.

The English trader Archibald Little, noting his expenses for a night's stay in the Treaty Port, showed how far four English pennies went in late 19th-century Yichang, and incidentally his solicitude for his servant:

Supper for self and coolie, 4 bowls of rice at 10 cash (copper cash),
  'fixings' of cabbage and bean curd free ......................... 40
Use of straw-plaited mattress for ditto, 2 at 10 ...................... 20
Breakfast, same as supper ......................................... 40
Supper and breakfast for 'Nigger', my dog ......................... 20
Pair of straw sandals for coolie (his old ones being worn out) .......... 12
Total 132 copper cash, or, in English money, 4d .................... 132

During the warlord years of the early part of this century, Yichang's revenue was greatly boosted by taxes imposed on boats carrying homegrown opium from Yunnan and Guizhou Provinces by its Opium Suppression Bureau.

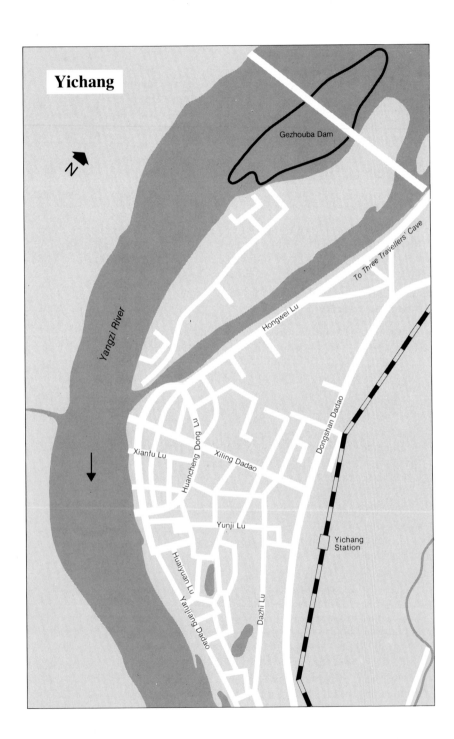

Yichang

Gezhouba Dam

Yangzi River

To Three Travellers' Cave

Hongwei Lu

Dongshan Dadao

Xianfu Lu

Huancheng Dong Lu

Xiling Dadao

Yunji Lu

Yichang
Station

Huaiyuan Lu

Yanjiang Dadao

Dazhi Lu

When Wuhan fell to the Japanese in 1938, Yichang became the centre for shipping essential personnel, machinery, libraries and museum collections up the Yangzi to Chongqing. After the Battle of Yichang in 1940, the Japanese used Yichang as a staging area for bombing raids over Chongqing.

## What to See in Yichang

The streets of the old town centre are lined with trees. Though the city wall was pulled down in 1929, the street names still indicate where it once stood (Eastern Ring Road, Southern Ring Road etc.). The main market is found just off Jiefang Lu. Along the waterfront a few old foreign buildings of the Treaty Port days can be seen.

Tourists may also visit, apart from the Gezhouba Dam, the **Three Travellers Cave**, ten kilometres (six miles) northwest of the city. In 819, three Tang-Dynasty poets, Bai Zhuyi, his brother Bai Xingjian, and Yuan Zhen, met up in Yichang and made an excursion to this site. While enjoying the spectacular scenery, they inscribed some poems on the cave walls. Afterwards they were dubbed the 'First Three Travellers'.

In the Song Dynasty (960–1279) the famous literary family of Su — father and two sons — on their way to the capital to take the imperial examinations, visited the cave and added poems as well. All three passed the imperial examinations at the same time. People call these gentlemen the 'Second Three Travellers'.

Throughout the ages, other visiting literati and officials have left their contributions on the cave walls.

A small spring trickles through the rock near the entrance; local superstition maintains that if women wash their hands in its pure water it will improve their culinary skills.

The hill above the cave presents a fine view of the entrance to Xiling Gorge. The Zixi Pavilion contains a memorial stone to the 11th-century philosopher Ouyang Xiu, who lived in Yichang for three years. Nearby is a drum platform said to be the site where Zhang Fei, a general of the State of Shu (third century), beat his battle drums.

Visitors are usually taken on a short excursion along a mountain road offering stunning views of Xiling Gorge, and passing several peaks, including Filial Mountain and Camel Mountain. The road continues over a natural stone bridge, which was originally — so legend has it — a fairy's silken sash, thrown up to help her mortal husband ascend to heaven with her. The stone gateway and its steep stone steps delineate the ancient land route crossed by travellers to western Hubei and Sichuan.

Below Yichang lies the bluff known as Tiger's Teeth Gorge which, to upriver travellers, is their first glimpse of the sights to come.

# The Middle Reaches

From Yichang the Yangzi enters its middle basin, flowing for 1,010 kilometres (630 miles) to the mouth of Boyang Lake in Jiangxi Province. The river, widening out abruptly from the narrow confines of Xiling Gorge and with a pent-up force out of Gezhouba Dam, rolls through broad floodplains, fed by tributaries and lakes that become serious flood points during heavy summer rains.

Networks of dikes and embankments — obscuring the view — stretch the length of the river, which can be as wide as one and a half to two kilometres (one to 1.3 miles), and can even today cause widespread flooding during normal rainy seasons. In abnormal summer deluges the many lakes in the area, joining forces with the Yangzi and its tributaries, inundate the land, forming great expanses of water. This must have been the situation observed by two great foreign travellers in China: Marco Polo in the 13th century and the French Lazarist priest, Abbé Huc, in the 18th century, both of whom recorded the Yangzi as being more than 15 kilometres (nine miles) wide.

Up to the Sui Dynasty (581–618) the middle reaches were sparsely inhabited, but from the Tang Dynasty (618–907) on, waves of people migrated from the north, fleeing from civil wars, famines, heavy taxation and harassment from marauding Tibetans and Turks. With the sharp rise in population, dike construction became more intense. But it was during the Ming and Qing Dynasties that treasury funds were

allocated to the construction of dikes — mainly along the north bank of the Yangzi — which were built as high as 10–16 metres (33–52 feet) in places. Once built, the burden of maintenance fell to local landowners and peasants, and upkeep was often neglected.

The meandering, looping course of the river creates severe silting so that the raised riverbed requires constant dredging, and as large boats crisscross the channel, their wash churns into the embankment causing mini-landslides.

The rich alluvial Jianghan Plain, between the north bank of the Yangzi and the Han River, is a major cotton- and grain-growing area very vulnerable to flooding. In 1952 the Jingjiang Flood Diversion Project was launched. Flood prevention measures included the strengthening of the 180-kilometre (110-mile) stretch of dike along the Yangzi's northern bank (in the Shashi region), and the construction of flood intake sluices, regulating dams and retention basins on the south side to divert the waters. On the Han River, the Danjiangkou Water Conservancy Project and dam draw the flood waters from this tributary to irrigate the more arid regions of northwest Hubei. The Shashi retention basin, covering an area of 920 square kilometres (355 square miles), took 300,000 workers some 75 days to construct in 1954.

Above Dongting Lake, the Yangzi forms the border between the provinces of Hubei and Hunan. The lake is the second largest in China. Fed by four rivers and emptying its waters into the Yangzi, it abounds in aquatic products. At Dongting Lake the river streaks northeastwards, beside hinterland dotted with numerous lakes, towards Wuhan, the largest city along its middle reaches. Here it is joined by the 1,532-kilometre (952-mile) long Han River.

During the dry winters, shifting sandbars and low water levels pose serious hazards to shipping. At Wuhan, the navigation channel can be as shallow as two metres (6.5 feet). Estimates put the volume of silt passing Wuhan each year at more than 140 million cubic metres (183 million cubic yards).

Freshwater fish abound — silver and big-head carp, Yangzi sturgeon, Wuchang fish, and giant salamander, to name a few. Native to the river are dolphins and a species of alligator, though both of these are today extremely rare indeed.

Having crossed the entire width of Hubei Province, the river enters Jiangxi, forming its border with Anhui. Immediately below the city of Jiujiang and the cherished, beautiful mountain of Lushan, it is joined by the blue freshwaters of Boyang Lake, the biggest in all of China. From here on, the Yangzi enters its lower reaches.

The river traffic is light, mostly convoys of barges or boats linked to a single tugboat, dredgers excavating the navigational channels, and fishing sampans with patched sails.

Steamer ferries stop briefly at the coal-mining town of **Zicheng** and pass under one of the few bridges that span the Yangzi.

## Jingzhou

Jingzhou, previously the famous city of Jiangling, has now been somewhat absorbed by the growth of Shashi. It is still surrounded by its 16-kilometre (ten-mile) long and nine-metre (30-foot) high city wall. Jingzhou is visited from Shashi.

Jingzhou was the capital of Jing, one of the nine great regions into which Emperor Yu, founder of the Xia Dynasty (2205–1766 BC), divided China. From Jingzhou the emperor received as tribute exotic gifts of gold, ivory, cinnabar, silver and feathers.

In the Spring and Autumn period (770–476 BC) the city was the capital of the Kingdom of Chu. Its walls, according to tradition, were first built in the third century by Guan Yu, a sworn brother of the King of Chu. Guan Yu was renowned for his strength, height and valour. A thousand years after his death he was deified as the God of War, and his fierce black-faced image appears in many Chinese temples throughout Asia. Stories of his exploits and battles over the city are vividly told in the novel, *Romance of the Three Kingdoms*.

As Jingzhou was the capital of 20 kingdoms during the Spring and Autumn and Warring States periods, it is not surprising that valuable artifacts have been found buried in the many tombs on Phoenix Hill. These relics, in particular an important collection of lacquerware, 2,000 year-old silk garments and fabrics, and an almost perfectly preserved male corpse of a Han-Dynasty official, are exhibited at the Jingzhou Museum. The museum is one of the best in all of China as well as an important research centre, and is well worth a visit.

## Shashi

Shashi is situated on the north bank of the Yangzi, and its cotton mills are supplied with raw cotton from the rich Jianghan Plain on which it stands. Shashi's population of 240,000 is principally employed in its many light industrial enterprises — machinery, durable consumer goods, printing, and dyeing and textiles.

The city was the port for the ancient city of Jiangling (Jingzhou) and a distribution centre for produce from surrounding towns and Dongting Lake which was transshipped mostly to Wuhan. This trade was in cotton, beans, grain and aquatic products. In the Tang Dynasty (618–907) it already enjoyed a reputation as a prosperous city, but its peak was reached during the years of the Taiping Rebellion, in the mid-19th century. After the rebels captured Nanjing in 1853, river

trade on the Yangzi between Shashi and Shanghai more or less came to
a standstill, so Shashi became vital to the distribution of products
coming downriver from Sichuan.

The Sino-Japanese Treaty of 1895 opened the city to foreign trade;
Japanese engaged in the cotton-seed trade formed the majority of the
resident foreigners, though this community was never large.

There is a story that the army of Communist General Ho Lung
captured Swedish missionaries here in 1931. The women were released
following negotiations with the Swedish Consul-General, but the
release of a doctor was delayed until a ransom was paid. The ransom
demanded was: four dozen Parker fountain pens, four dozen watches
and 60 or 70 cases of medical drugs!

West of the city, the seven-storeyed **Wanshoubao Pagoda**, built in
the Ming Dynasty, stands directly on the waterfront. Bas-relief figures
of Buddha, set into niches, and inscriptions by the donors adorn its
brick façade. A monastery once adjoined it.

Tourist boats frequently stop in Shashi so that a visit can be paid to
the ancient walled city of Jingzhou nearby.

Below Shashi the river winds tortuously towards Dongting Lake for
about 320 kilometres (200 miles). Villages dot the south bank of the
river and water buffalo graze in the paddy fields. The north
embankment is often too high for a view of the surrounding country.

## Dongting Lake

The beautiful Dongting Lake is rich in fairy tales and legends. On its
eastern shore stands the graceful three-storey **Yueyang Tower** of
Yueyang City, one of the Three Great Towers south of the Yangzi (the
other two being Yellow Crane Tower in Wuchang, and Prince Teng
Pavilion in Nanchang). From its terraces and from pleasures boats on
the lake, many famous Chinese poets have been moved to verse.

> The lake embraces distant hills and devours the Yangzi,
>    its mighty waves rolling endlessly.
> From morning glow to evening light, the views change a thousand,
>    ten thousand times.
> On top of the tower the mind relaxes, the heart delights.
> All honours and disgrace are forgotten.
> What pleasure, what joy to sit here and drink in the breeze.
>                              Fan Zhongyan (989–1052)

Said to have been constructed on the site of a reviewing platform for
navy manoeuvres on the lake during the third century, the first tower
was erected in 716. The present golden-tiled, square tower dates from
1985, but it has been rebuilt in the Song-Dynasty style at great
expense.

Legend has it that the tower was saved from collapse by the supernatural powers of Lu Dongbin, a Daoist Immortal, who also got drunk here three times. These occasions are remembered in the form of the Thrice Drunken Pavilion, which flanks the tower.

An excursion on to the lake can be made to **Junshan Island**, 15 kilometres (nine miles) away. Some 4,000 years ago, Emperor Shun, on an inspection tour, died at Mount Jiuyi on the south bank of the lake. Two of his devoted concubines, hurrying to his side, became stranded on Junshan Island. The story goes that in their distress, their copious tears blotted the local bamboo, henceforth known as the Spotted Bamboo of Junshan. They drowned themselves in the lake, and their graves remain.

In 219 BC, Emperor Qin Shihuangdi, also on a tour of the Dongting, was delayed at Junshan Island by a sudden storm. When he consulted his geomancer as to whether spirits were impeding his progress, he was told of the concubines' graves. In a fury he ordered the burning of the island and had five stone seals placed there, forbidding its name to be used or anyone to visit it.

On the 100-hectare (250-acre) island, the Junshan Silver Needle Tea is grown, so highly prized that it was once presented as a tribute to the imperial court.

Once China's largest freshwater lake, the Dongting now ranks second, due to sandbars and silt accumulation from the four rivers which feed into it. As a result of flood prevention schemes — 6,100 irrigation and drainage channels and 15,000 sluices — the surrounding land has become productive all year round and the lake acts as a reservoir for summer flood waters. The 3,000-square kilometre (1,160-square mile) lake abounds in fish.

Luxury goods from Canton — from pearls to kingfisher feathers — reached the ancient capitals by way of the Xiang River, through Dongting Lake, along the Yangzi down to Yangzhou and then on up the Grand Canal.

## Three Kingdoms' Red Cliff

From the flat bank appears a sharp rock escarpment dotted with pavilions and paths. This is the site of the great Battle of the Red Cliff between the huge forces of Cao Cao of Wei and the combined, lesser armies of Shu and Wu in 208.

Cao Cao had consolidated the power of the Kingdom of Wei in the north and sought to extend it to the Yangzi. His troops, all from the northern plains, were not accustomed to naval warfare. Nevertheless, he took his army of 200,000 men to launch his attack on the Kingdom of Shu, whose king, Liu Bei, called upon the King of Wu for assistance.

In urgent need of 100,000 arrows to repel the invaders, Zhuge Liang (adviser to Liu Bei) devised a brilliant stratagem. Twenty naval junks, beating war drums, but stacked high with only bundles of straw shrouded in black cloth, feigned an advance on the Wei encampment on a dark, foggy night. The Wei commanders responded by discharging their arrows into the indistinct hulks on the junks. By dawn, each junk bristled with thousands of arrows, more than enough for the army's requirements.

By another ruse, Cao Cao was persuaded by a spy in his camp to secure all his boats together for a forthcoming attack, so that his soldiers would feel as if they were on firm ground. The armies of Wu and Shu set fire to the boats in the midst of the battle and, with a favourable wind, the great conflagration brought about the defeat of Cao Cao, who fled northwards.

Red Cliff itself is said to have been forever scorched red by the flames of this day-long battle. In a victory celebration, General Zhou Yu of Wu, flourishing his writing brush, jubilantly inscribed the gigantic characters 'Red Cliff' (Chi Bi) on the cliff face, which can be seen to this day.

Pavilions on the hill commemorate specific incidents in the battle, and there is an exhibition of over 2,000 weapons, dating from the Three Kingdoms period, that were found in the area.

The story of the battle is known to all Chinese, and this makes the site a very popular tourist spot.

## Han River

The Han River, the Yangzi's longest tributary (1,532 kilometres, or 952 miles), rises in the Qingling Mountains of Shaanxi Province. In 1488 it changed its course, separating the city of Hanyang from the fishing village of Hankou, as it then was. Though dikes line much of its lower course, this stretch has a history of frequent flooding. The British consular officer, August R. Margary, who travelled all the way from Shanghai up the Yangzi and on to the Burmese border in 1876, only to be murdered by tribesmen as he crossed back into China, wrote of Hankou:

This year they have had no inundation, but it is of almost annual occurrence. Even at Hankow the foreign settlement is frequently submerged. The river rises six feet above the level of the fine stone bund they have made there, and quietly takes possession of all the lower rooms in the noble-looking mansions which the merchants occupy. All their dining-room furniture has to be removed above. Boats become the only means of locomotion, and ladies can be seen canoeing in and out of their houses, and over the bund where they are wont to promenade at other times.

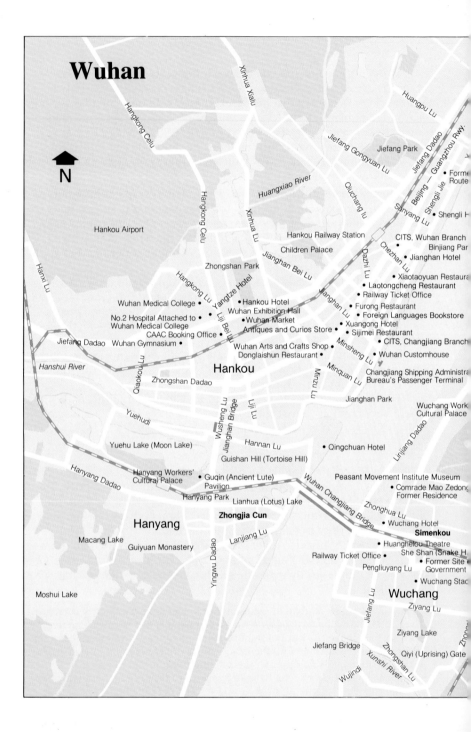

# Wuhan

N

Xinhua Xialu

Hangkong Celu

Huangpu Lu

Jiefang Gongyuan Lu

Jiefang Park

Jiefang Dadao — Guangzhou Rwy.

Beijing — Guangzhou Rwy.

Shengli Jie

Forme
Route

Huangxiao River

Qiuchang lu

Sanyang Lu

Shengli H

Hankou Airport

Hangkong Celu

Xinhua Lu

Hankou Railway Station

Children Palace

CITS, Wuhan Branch

Chezhan Lu

Binjiang Par

Jianghan Hotel

Jianghan Bei Lu

Zhongshan Park

Dazhi Lu

Xiaotaoyuan Restaura

Laotongcheng Restaurant

Railway Ticket Office

Hangkong Lu

Yangtze Hotel

Wuhan Medical College

Hankou Hotel

Jianghan Lu

Furong Restaurant

Wuhan Exhibition Hall

Foreign Languages Bookstore

No.2 Hospital Attached to
Wuhan Medical College

Liji Bei Lu

Wuhan Market

Xuangong Hotel

CAAC Booking Office

Antiques and Curios Store

Sijimei Restaurant

Jiefang Dadao   Wuhan Gymnasium

Wuhan Arts and Crafts Shop

Minsheng Lu

CITS, Changjiang Branch

Hanxi Lu

Donglaishun Restaurant

Wuhan Customhouse

Hanshui River

**Hankou**

Minquan Lu

Changjiang Shipping Administra
Bureau's Passenger Terminal

Qiaokou Lu

Zhongshan Dadao

Minzu Lu

Jianghan Park

Wuchang Work
Cultural Palace

Yuehudi

Wusheng Lu

Jianghan Bridge

Liji Lu

Linjiang Dadao

Yuehu Lake (Moon Lake)

Hannan Lu

Qingchuan Hotel

Guishan Hill (Tortoise Hill)

Hanyang Dadao

Hanyang Workers'
Cultural Palace

Guqin (Ancient Lute)
Pavilion

Wuhan Changjiang Bridge

Peasant Movement Institute Museum

Comrade Mao Zedong
Former Residence

Hanyang Park

Lianhua (Lotus) Lake

Zhonghua Lu

**Zhongjia Cun**

Wuchang Hotel

**Hanyang**

Lanjiang Lu

**Simenkou**

Macang Lake

Yingwu Dadao

Guiyuan Monastery

Huanghelou Theatre

Railway Ticket Office

She Shan (Snake H

Pengliuyang Lu

Former Site
Government

Moshui Lake

Wuchang Stac

Jiefang Lu

**Wuchang**

Ziyang Lu

Ziyang Lake

Jiefang Bridge

Zhongshan Lu

Qiyi (Uprising) Gate

Wujindi

Xunshi River

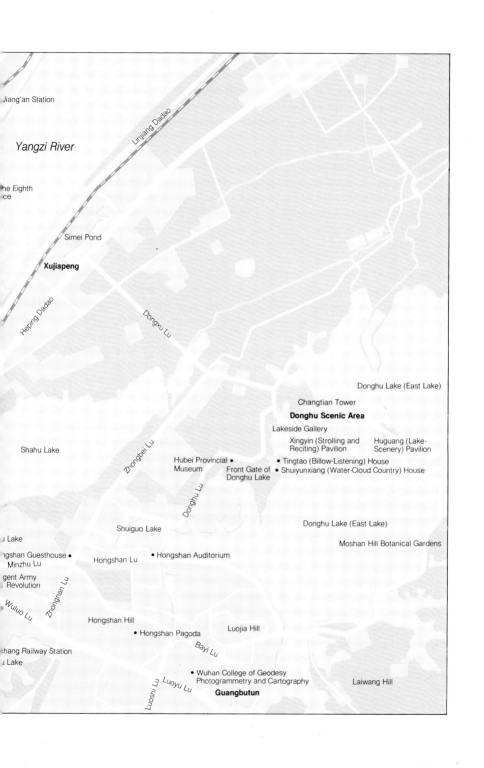

Jiang'an Station

*Yangzi River*

Linjiang Dadao

he Eighth
ce

Simei Pond

**Xujiapeng**

Heping Dadao

Dongxu Lu

Donghu Lake (East Lake)

Changtian Tower

**Donghu Scenic Area**

Lakeside Gallery

Xingyin (Strolling and      Huguang (Lake-
Reciting) Pavilion        Scenery) Pavilion

Shahu Lake

Zhongbei Lu

Hubei Provincial •
Museum        Front Gate of
Donghu Lake

• Tingtao (Billow-Listening) House
• Shuiyunxiang (Water-Cloud Country) House

Donghu Lu

Shuiguo Lake

Donghu Lake (East Lake)

Moshan Hill Botanical Gardens

u Lake

ngshan Guesthouse •
Minzhu Lu

Hongshan Lu      • Hongshan Auditorium

gent Army
Revolution

Zhongnan Lu

Wuluo Lu

Hongshan Hill

• Hongshan Pagoda

Luojia Hill

Bayi Lu

shang Railway Station
u Lake

Luoshi Lu

Luoyu Lu

• Wuhan College of Geodesy
Photogrammetry and Cartography

**Guangbutun**

Laiwang Hill

Flooding occurred 11 times from 1931 to 1949; in 1931 and 1935 boats sailed down the streets of Wuhan. Though much has been done in recent years to control the Han's waters, the danger is still very real.

# Wuhan

The vast triple-metropolis of Wuhan, capital of Hubei Province, sprawls along both sides of the Yangzi. On the north bank are the twin cities of Hankou and Hanyang, divided by the Han River. On the south side lies Wuchang. Wuhan, with a population of 3.7 million, is the largest industrial and trading city in central China. The Beijing– Canton Railway cuts through the city, adding to its importance as a hub of both land and water communications.

Though some of the passenger boats from Chongqing continue down to Shanghai, Wuhan is the terminus for most of the Yangzi Gorges cruises. Larger boats ply the Wuhan–Shanghai leg. We have an account by George E. Morrison, the illustrious correspondent of *The Times* of London, on the first leg of his journey up the river — from Shanghai to Wuhan — in 1894.

I travelled as a Chinese, dressed in warm Chinese clothing, with a pigtail attached to the inside of my hat. I could not have been more comfortable. I had a small cabin to myself. I had of course my own bedding, and by paying a Mexican dollar a day to the Chinese steward, 'foreign chow' was brought me from the saloon. The traveller who cares to travel in this way, to put his pride in his pocket and a pigtail down his back, need pay only one-fourth of what it would cost him to travel as a European in European dress.

The city's iron and steel works are some of the largest in the country. Cotton and textile mills and industrial machine-building have replaced the tea trade as Wuhan's economic base. Research institutes based here are studying the Yangzi's potential in the fields of water conservancy, navigation, hydroelectric power, control of pollution, and aquatic products.

Wuhan, along with Chongqing and Nanjing, is one of the 'three furnaces of China', with summer temperatures in the long summer months well into the 30s (°C) (80s °F).

The huge bridge, over one and a half kilometres (one mile) long, which spans the Yangzi and connects the cities, was built in 1957 on two levels, one for the railway and one for motor traffic.

## *History of Wuhan*

The area on which Wuhan stands was settled in the first century; in the third century it was part of the Kingdom of Wu. Wuchang is the oldest of the three cities. By the Yuan Dynasty (1279–1368) it was the capital of the region and was enclosed by a city wall until the end of the 19th century. Hanyang was founded in the Sui Dynasty (581–618) and remained a small walled city until a farsighted official of the Qing Dynasty (1644–1911), Zhang Zhidong, established factories and an arsenal there in the 1890s. Hankou was only a fishing village until the 19th century.

It is, however, the city of Hankou which is best known to foreigners, for after it was declared a Treaty Port in 1861 it became a major centre of the tea trade and the focal point of the annual China Tea Races.

**Hankow Tea Races** The handsome, full-sailed tea clippers which plied the high seas between China and Britain from the 18th to the 19th century were initially confined to the coastal ports — first Canton, then Shanghai and eventually Fuzhou. As the British East India Company lost its monopoly and the tea trade gathered momentum, so did the competition between shipping companies, particularly as the quality of the tea could deteriorate on a long sea journey. The fastest ships charged the highest freight rates in this lucrative trade. This was the origin of the annual China Tea Races, first in elegant clippers and later in the early steamships.

Following the opening of the Yangzi River cities to foreign trade after the 1858 Treaty of Tientsin, the first tea clipper, the *Challenger*, reached Hankou in 1861.

The introduction of the steamship in the middle of the 19th century saw an end to these romantic sailing ships, and the opening of the Suez Canal in 1869 greatly reduced the sailing time. Nevertheless, the Hankow (Hankou) Tea Races continued.

Each May, tea buyers, known as *chazi*, came to Hankou as the ships began to arrive from England, Russia and America. The Hankow (Hankou) Club sprang to life, with the Russian *chazi* drinking only champagne throughout the season. As many as 16 or 17 vessels would make up the British fleet, of which only two or three would be hot favourites and allowed to charge the highest freight rates.

Loaded with their cargo of black and green tea, the race began. The first leg from Hankou to the Red Buoy at Wusong (near Shanghai) could take as little as 36 hours if the ships did not run aground; then down the South China Sea to Singapore, where time was always lost in stockpiling coal for the last leg to London. In the 1877 race, two ships passed the Red Buoy together and reached Singapore with only 1 hour and 40 minutes between them. One ship lost six hours in port and arrived in London only 23 hours behind the winner after an exciting voyage of 31 days.

As the first ships were sighted in the English Channel, word was sent to the London brokers who would rush to the docks as the vessels berthed. In great excitement the tea chests were broken open for samples which were hurried off for inspection by the various buyers.

By the late 1880s India had moved into the lead of tea-exporting countries. The collapse of the China tea market brought about the end of a romantic era.

**Foreign Concessions** There were five settlements — British, Russian, French, German and Japanese — situated side by side along the north embankment of the Yangzi. Oceangoing steamers from New York, Odessa and London anchored at its docks. Until the foreign import of opium ceased in the first decade of this century, opium-laden ships sailed up the river as far as Hankou.

Life in the foreign concessions was similar to that of Shanghai. Horseracing was popular, with Hankou boasting two racecourses, one for Chinese and one for foreigners. There was even a golf course, while the Recreation Club was considered by many to be the best in China at that time.

In the 1911 Revolution, much of Hankou was burnt to the ground during clashes between the revolutionaries and imperial troops.

After the fall of the capital, Nanjing, in 1937 to the Japanese during the Sino-Japanese War, the Guomindang government made Wuhan its capital for a year, before moving to Chongqing. In the 1938 assault on Wuhan, casualty figures were in the tens of thousands.

The Communist Party was very active in Wuhan before 1949,

organizing railway strikes and peasant training programmes. It was here that Chairman Mao, at the age of 73, took his famous 15-kilometre (nine-mile) swim in the Yangzi during the Cultural Revolution days of 1966.

## *What to See in Wuhan*

## Hankou

Hankou is the main commercial area of Wuhan. Between its long main shopping street, Zhongshan Dadao, and the high embankment along the river are numerous street markets. The old foreign concessions line the embankment for three kilometres (two miles) and this area is still very much intact. The vicinity of Hankou Railway Station is always busy and provides an interesting walk. The old Customs House on the waterfront is a distinctive landmark. Jiefang Park and Zhongshan Park, across the railway line, are the sites of the former racecourses.

## Hanyang

### Lute Platform (Guqin Tai)

Opposite Tortoise Hill, which overlooks the Han River, is the Hanyang Workers Cultural Palace Gardens, encompassing the charming Lute Platform, a small complex of courtyards, pavilions and

gardens enclosed by a tiled wall. It was built in commemoration of two musicians, Yu Baiya and Zhong Ziqi, who lived 2,000 years ago. While visiting Hanyang, Yu played his lute but only Zhong understood and appreciated his performance. They became fast friends and arranged to meet again at the same time the following year. Yu returned only to find that his friend had died. At Zhong's grave, Yu played a farewell song and, vowing never again to use the instrument, broke its strings.

The Lute Platform is now a haven for Chinese opera lovers (mostly men) who gather on Sunday mornings to sip tea and listen to the performers. In the gardens, *wushu* (martial arts) and *taijiquan* exercise classes are held. Paintings by local artists are on exhibition and for sale in the main hall. Nearby is a Qing memorial stone dedicated to the lutanist.

### Guiyuan Monastery
This fine Zen Buddhist monastery on Cuiwei Lu, where monks from the surrounding provinces gathered to study the scriptures, is 300 years old. The striking architectural complex includes Drum and Bell Towers, temple halls, the Luohan Hall and the Lotus Pond. The Luohan Hall contains 500 gold-painted wooden statues of Buddhist monk-saints; no two are the same. It is said the two sculptors employed on this task took nine years to complete it. The monastery runs a vegetarian restaurant, the Yunjizhai, for visitors.

## Wuchang

### Yellow Crane Tower
On Snake Hill is the site of the ancient Yellow Crane Tower, widely celebrated by Chinese poets throughout the ages. The legend concerns a Daoist sage who flew away on a yellow crane to become an Immortal. The tower has been rebuilt many times. Beside the new Yellow Crane Tower (completed in 1986) is a White Dagoba which dates from the Yuan Dynasty (1279–1368).

### Headquarters of the 1911 Revolution
Known as the Red House, this building on Shouyi Lu was the headquarters of the 1911 Revolution against the Manchu Qing Dynasty, led by Dr Sun Yatsen. Today, the building, in front of which stands a statue of Sun, is a museum to that revolution.

### Peasant Movement Institute Museum
Mao Zedong directed this institute in the late 1920s. Its object was to train men to organize the peasants into associations and underground activities.

**East Lake**
A large scenic area, in the eastern suburbs of Wuchang, is centred on
East Lake. Around its shores are numerous pavilions and halls,
including a memorial to the third-century BC poet Qu Yuan (see page
76) and a monument to nine heroines who died fighting the Manchu
troops during the Taiping Rebellion in the 19th century. A low
causeway leads to Moshan Hill and its botanical gardens with views
across the city and the beautiful countryside.

**Hubei Provincial Museum**
Off Donghu Lu, near East Lake, this small museum has a rich
collection of artifacts excavated in the province. Of special interest is a
display of finds from the tomb of the Marquis Yi of Zeng of the
Warring States period (475−221 BC). Among them is a set of 65
bronze chime bells. Replicas of these have been made and concerts of
ancient music are given by a special chime-bells orchestra under the
auspices of the Hubei Provincial Museum and Art Institute of Wuhan.
The second floor of the museum is devoted to the province's
revolutionary history.

## Dongpo Red Cliff

On the north bank of the Yangzi, just west of Huangzhou city, is the
Red Cliff of Su Dongpo. On its summit are pavilions and halls
dedicated to one of China's great poets, Su Dongpo (1037−1101).
Having passed the imperial examinations at the young age of 20, he
held various important scholarly posts in the Northern Song capital of
Kaifeng but fell from grace when he criticized some new law reforms.
After arrest and imprisonment, he was demoted to the status of
assistant commissioner to the Huangzhou militia. He lived in
considerable hardship with his household of 20 members, tilling a few
acres of land himself. The Red Cliff became one of his favourite
haunts, and he and his guests, boating beneath the cliff, would
compose poetry, drink wine, admire the moon and carouse all night
long. In the Qing Dynasty (1644−1911) this cliff was named Dongpo
Red Cliff to distinguish it from the other Red Cliff that was the scene
of a battle in the Three Kingdoms period (see page 92). The Qing-
Dynasty halls contain examples of Su Dongpo's beautiful calligraphy,
poems, essays and paintings carved on both stone and wooden tablets.

## Qizhou

About one hour's sailing east of **Huangshi**, the industrial and iron ore
mining city below Wuhan, is the small town of Qizhou. Though it has a

history of 1,000 years, it is famous as the home town of Li Shizhen (1518–93), a Ming-Dynasty herbalist and physician.

After practising Chinese medicine in his youth, Li spent 30 years rewriting and categorizing ancient Chinese medical books, travelling far and wide in search of specimens. His treatise formed 52 scrolls, with almost 2,000 entries. Sadly, he died before receiving recognition. However, his son presented a copy of Li's work to Emperor Wanli (1573–1620), a patron of scholarship. The emperor, much pleased with the work, ordered its wide distribution.

Li Shizhen's classical works are the basis of traditional Chinese medical practice today and have been translated into a number of foreign languages.

The graves of Li Shizhen and his wife are situated at Rain Lake, north of the town, surrounded by gardens of medicinal herbs.

The local bamboo is used for making summer bed mats, and flutes made from this bamboo were widely praised as early as the Tang Dynasty. Qizhou's White Flower Snake medicine is supposed to relieve rheumatic pains, while its Green Hairy-backed Turtles are used in medicines that allegedly cure tuberculosis and body fluid deficiencies.

About halfway between Qizhou and Jiujiang, the river leaves Hubei Province and thenceforth marks the provincial boundary between Hubei to the north and Jiangxi to the south as far as the mouth of Boyang Lake.

## Jiujiang

Though the capital of Jiangxi Province is Nanchang, further south, Jiujiang, with a population of 355,000, is the main port for distributing products from Boyang Lake and the surrounding counties as well as much of the chinaware produced at the porcelain capital of Jingdezhen. It has the reputation of being the hottest port on the Yangzi, with extremely oppressive summers. Though once an important tea-buying centre in its own right, it was gradually superseded by Wuhan, and tea grown in Jiangxi was shipped either upstream to Wuhan or downstream to Shanghai. Today, cotton textiles form Jiujiang's main industry.

Jiujiang is the main access city to one of China's most famous mountain beauty spots, Lushan, lying only a short distance to the south, which attracts 2.5 million tourists a year.

### *History of Jiujiang*

In ancient times, nine rivers were said to have converged at this point, hence the name Jiujiang — 'Nine Rivers' — though it was also called

Jiangzhou and Xunyang. In its long history it has seen many upheavals; in the last century it was a Taiping stronghold from which the rebels held out against the imperial Qing armies for five years.

The area holds many memories for lovers of Chinese poetry. Tao Yuanming (365−429) lived at the foot of Lushan and was appointed magistrate of nearby Pengze County. This post was so poorly endowed that, rather than work 'for five pecks of grain to break one's back', he resigned after 83 days, preferring to eke out a living as a recluse in his home village. His essay *Peach Flower Garden* depicts his idea of a perfect society. Li Bai (701−62), implicated in the An Lushan Rebellion, was imprisoned briefly in Jiujiang in 757. Bai Juyi (772−846) also spent a period of official disgrace here as a middle-ranking official and is affectionately remembered. His poem *The Lute Song* tells of his sadness at his isolation in this small town. Su Dongpo was a frequent visitor to the area.

When Jiujiang was thrown open as a Treaty Port in 1861 it had suffered terribly as a consequence of the Taiping Rebellion (1851−64). A British member of Lord Elgin's mission noted in 1858:

We found it to the last degree deplorable. A single dilapidated street, composed only of a few mean shops, was all that existed of this once thriving and populous city: the remainder of the vast area, comprised within walls five or six miles in circumference, contained nothing but ruins, weeds, and kitchen gardens.

Jiujiang was once one of the three centres of the tea trade in China, along with Hankou and Fuzhou. There were two Russian factories producing brick-tea, but these ceased to operate after 1917. The British concession in Jiujiang was given up in 1927 after looting by mutineering garrisons and mobs.

## What to See in Jiujiang

Sycamore trees line the streets of Jiujiang. The old downtown area is not large, sandwiched between Gantang Lake and the river bank. The old foreign concession area abuts the river-steamer dock and some old buildings remain — a church, the old French hospital and the Council House (now the Bank of China).

Crunchy, sweet Jiujiang tea biscuits made from tea oil, sesame and orange osmanthus flower originated in the Song Dynasty; so did the local wine, Fenggang Jiu, made from glutinous rice and fermented in sealed vats for five years.

### Gantang Lake and Yanshui Pavilion

Gantang Lake is divided into two by a dike and bridge built in 821. The Sixian Bridge, now enlarged, still stands on the causeway which

one crosses to reach Yangyue Pavilion on the low hill overlooking the
lake. It is well stocked with silver and grass carp, and seagulls skim its
surface. It is said that in the Three Kingdoms period the Eastern Wu
general, Zhou Yu, inspected his warships from a reviewing platform on
the lake, traces of which remain.

Linked to the shore by a zigzag bridge is the pretty Yanshui (Misty
Water) Pavilion. A pavilion was first built here in the Tang Dynasty
(618–907) by the poet Bai Juyi during his unhappy posting in Jiujiang.
It was named the Drenched Moon Pavilion after a line from one of his
poems: 'Bidding farewell, I saw the moon drenched by the river.' In
the Northern Song period (960–1127) a highly regarded Neo-
Confucian philosopher, Zhou Dun, taught in Jiujiang and his son built
a pavilion on the lake to his father's memory, calling it Yanshui
Pavilion. The present island pavilion dates from the late Qing period.
One small hall is dedicated to Bai Juyi, and other rooms display local
archaeological discoveries. The city's antiques store is located here.

**Nengren Temple**
The Qing halls here are the oldest buildings left in Jiujiang, although
the temple was established earlier, in the sixth century. Three or four
monks and several nuns tend the temple. The seven-storey **Great
Victory Pagoda**, beside the temple, dates from the Song period
(960–1279).

## Suojiang Pagoda

This sexagonal seven-storey pagoda, overlooking the Yangzi embankment to the northeast of the city, was built in 1585. Damage to the 35-metre (115-foot) high pagoda caused by shelling from Japanese gunboats in the Second World War is still visible.

## Lang Jing (Wave Well)

In Yuliang Bei Lu near the waterfront is a small ancient well with a quaint history. Dug early in the Han Dynasty (206 BC−AD 220), it connected with the Yangzi so that when a wind created waves on the river the surface of the well water would ripple too. The well became clogged and disused over the years until it was rediscovered in the third century, and the original inscription and date were uncovered. This was such a good omen that the well was renamed Auspicious Well. The poet Li Bai in the eighth century referred to it as the Wave Well in one of his poems, as did Su Dongpo. Waves no longer appear on its surface but the well is still in use.

## Donglin Monastery

Twenty-two kilometres (13.5 miles) southwest of Jiujiang at the foot of Lushan is the Donglin (Eastern Forest) Monastery, built in 386 for the monk Hui Yuan (334−416), founder of the Pure Land Sect of Buddhism. Among his 123 disciples were an Indian and a Nepalese (his overgrown grave is behind the temple) who spent many years translating Buddhist scriptures. The monastery reached its zenith in the Tang Dynasty, with a vast library of scriptures and over 300 halls and residences. Seriously damaged during the Taiping Rebellion, the monastery was almost ruined in the Republican period (1911−49). Today there is a community of 20 monks who hold daily services in the temple halls. Behind the temple in a bamboo grove is the Well of Intelligence — from which every visitor is anxious for a sip. The Luohan Pine trees in the courtyard are said to have been planted by Hui Yuan himself. Hui Yuan is also said to have struck the ground with his staff, causing the Ancient Dragon Spring to gush forth, thus proving his right to establish himself here.

Nearby is the Xilin Pagoda, all that remains of an earlier monastery complex.

# Lushan

Lushan, in the vicinity of Jiujiang, has always been appreciated by the Chinese as a mountain of great beauty and as a haven from the intense humid heat of the Yangzi valley summers. Its views eastwards to Boyang Lake and northwards across the river are spectacular.

Since the downstream steamers usually disembark passengers in the small hours of the morning, it is possible to enjoy the sunrise as your vehicle ascends the hairpin bends on the 29-kilometre (18-mile) trip to the top of Lushan.

April and May are the best times to visit, when the hills are covered with wild azalea and peach blossoms, and waterfalls are myriad. In the enervating months of June, July and August, the average temperature on Lushan is a comfortable 23°C (73°F), and during this peak season 25,000 tourists visit each day. In autumn the numbers drop off markedly and one is able to enjoy the changing autumnal colours of the trees at leisure, though the waterfalls dry up.

The town of **Guling** was established at the end of the 19th century by foreign traders and missionaries as a summer retreat for their families from as far away as Shanghai. They built over 100 summer bungalows and an American hospital (now the Lushan Guesthouse). They would be carried by sedan chair along the narrow path up the mountainside. Chiang Kai-shek's summer house — Meilu Villa — is still there, as is his library which now houses the **Lushan Museum**. Beside this is **Lushan People's Theatre** where in 1959 the Communist Party of China held its eighth plenary session, known later as the Lushan Conference, which resulted in the dismissal of the People's Liberation Army Commander-in-Chief, Peng Dehuai. The **Botanical Garden** was established in 1934; it has more than 4,000 kinds of flowers, trees and other plants.

Strange rock shapes, sheer peaks (the highest — Dahanyang — is 1,543 metres, or 5,060 feet), steep cliffs, overhangs and caves, as well as a wide variety of lovely trees, are some of the splendours of Lushan. Its mystery is captured by Su Dongpo, who wrote:

It's a ridge when looked at face to face,
It's a peak when looked at sidewise;
It's always not the same when looked at from afar or near,
    when looked at from above or below.
You don't know what Lushan is really like,
Merely because you yourself are living in it.

Guesthouses and sanatoriums (over 1,000 of them) abound in the Guling valley.

Special Lushan dishes are the small Stone Fish from the Xilin River (best eaten in spring and autumn), Stone Ear (a black fungus), and Stone Chicken (a black-skinned frog found in the damp caves on Lushan, tasting rather like chicken and best eaten between June and September), as well as fish from Boyang Lake.

Lushan's Misty Cloud Green Tea (Yunwu Lu Cha), once sent as tribute to the emperors, should be sampled. The tea-leaves are processed seven times to obtain its special fragrance.

## Stone Bell Hill

By taking a small vehicular ferry across the mouth of Boyang Lake to Hukou, one may climb the small, 50-metre (165-foot) high Stone Bell Hill (Shizhong Shan) to which visitors have been coming for centuries. The hill overlooks the lake and the Yangzi River, and the meeting of the waters is clearly defined by an abrupt colour change. Mystery surrounds the strange bell-like sound which can be heard at Stone Bell Hill. There are three theories: that the hill is shaped like a bell and is hollow inside; that the rock, when struck, rings like a bell; or that the water, lapping into the nooks and crannies around the base, causes a bell-like sound. Su Dongpo made three special trips to try to solve the mystery, and having eventually settled on the last explanation, wrote an essay on the subject.

The present buildings date from the mid-19th century when the Taiping rebel commander Shi Dakai, choosing the mouth of the lake as a defensive position, built a stronghold on the hill, occupying it between 1853 and 1857. The Qing armies, miscalculating their enemy's strength, entered the lake in their war-junks, whereupon the Taipings stretched ropes across the lake mouth, dividing the Qing navy into two and routing them. The Qing general Zeng Guofan, utterly humiliated, attempted to drown himself but was rescued by his retinue. The remains of the Taiping army stronghold can still be seen, and a pavilion on the side of the hill contains a stone tablet dedicated by Zeng Guofan to those who lost their lives in that battle.

Peng Yulin, also a Qing general, later built a wonderful villa here with winding balconies, small ponds, carved pavilions and exquisite gardens. The lovely two-storeyed **Plum Flower Hall (Meihua Ting)** was erected in memory of the cultivated young woman he loved but could not marry. She died of a broken heart and he painted 11,000 pictures of plum flowers with her in mind.

This hill is also called the Lower Stone Bell Hill to distinguish it from the Upper Stone Bell Hill nearby. There is a delightful legend about the formation of these two small hills. The supreme Daoist deity, the Jade Emperor, instructed one of his officials to find two bells suitable for his palace. The official searched everywhere until he finally found two stone hills shaped like bells. He was delivering them to the palace when his carrying pole broke at the mouth of Boyang Lake; the stone hills fell to the ground and have remained there ever since.

## Dragon Palace Cave

Sixty-seven kilometres (42 miles) east of Jiujiang, this 1,700-metre (1,860-yard) long natural cave is in the scenic surroundings of Dark

Dragon Hill (Wulong Shan), in Pengze County, Jiangxi Province. This natural beauty spot comprises eight adjoining caverns with interior limestone formations resembling palace lanterns, dragon thrones, boats and other objects. One section is called the East Sea Dragon Palace after the classic 16th-century Chinese novel *Journey to the West* (sometimes known as *Monkey*). Coloured lighting heightens the effect.

## Boyang Lake

The surface area of China's largest freshwater lake is around 5,000 square kilometres (1,930 square miles), increasing in size during the flood season and shrinking in winter. Five rivers flow into the lake and eight counties border it. From ancient times, this fertile region has been one of the 'rice-bowls' of China. The Boyang teems with fish, such as mandarin, anchovy and whitebait. It continues to fulfil its age-old function as a transport link for local produce — grain, tea, silk, bamboo, and particularly the porcelain from the kaolin (white clay) potteries of Jingdezhen, which have been producing since the second century BC, and supplying the imperial court from the fifth century on.

The Yangzi, Boyang Lake and the Gan River formed a water link as far south as Canton.

A 22,000-hectare (54,000-acre) nature reserve has been established in the vicinity of Wucheng on the western side of the lake. It hosts Asia's greatest bird spectacle in winter, when over 4,000 cranes, 40,000 swan geese and around a quarter of a million ducks flock here. Over 90% of the world's population of the Siberian Crane winter at the reserve. Numbers have increased dramatically since the area became a protected reserve, with 1,700 birds counted in 1988.

Owing to the lake's strategic importance, numerous naval encounters took place on its waters. Emperor Wudi (reigned 420–3) was embattled here. It was the site of a decisive battle in the overthrow of the Yuan Dynasty in the 14th century. Another naval battle was fought between the Taiping rebels and the Qing imperial forces in 1855 (see page 109). Today, only graceful fishing boats in full sail occupy the lake.

Local fairy tales connect a small island in the lake, Shoe Hill or **Dagu Shan**, with the stories of Xiaogu Shan (see page 113) further downstream. It seems that Xiaogu Niang Niang and her betrothed escaped from her Emei Shan prison with the help of a precious umbrella. The pursuing Immortal, confronting them at Boyang Lake, threw his flying sword at the precious umbrella and in her confusion Xiaogu Niang Niang lost one of her embroidered slippers, which fell into the lake and was transformed into a shoe-shaped island.

# The Lower Reaches

The region around the lower Yangzi and its delta, the 'most prosperous in the country, is known as China's 'Land of Fish and Rice'.

From Hukou at the mouth of the Boyang, the Yangzi widens on its final sweep to the Yellow Sea, skirting northern Jiangxi and traversing the provinces of Anhui and Jiangsu. Hundreds of shallow lakes and streams, rich in freshwater crabs, prawns and fish, feed the river. From Nanjing downwards the river becomes tidal, and oceangoing vessels of 10,000 to 15,000 tons navigate its channels.

The deltaic plain of coastal Jiangsu — the most densely populated of China's provinces — is a veritable maze of natural waterways, man-made dikes and canals. Mulberry trees line their banks and humpbacked stone bridges link the picturesque towns and villages. These waterways serve as irrigation channels, drainage outlets and transport canals.

Three staple grain crops — two of paddy rice and one of winter wheat — are harvested each year. Since earliest times, sericulture has been an important economic factor, and though cotton replaced silk in importance after the 1930s, silkworm breeding is still a major home-industry and hard-cash earner for peasant families. Sericulture formed the basis on which the region's famous textile cities of Hangzhou, Suzhou, Wuxi, Nanjing and Shanghai were established.

Water conservancy plans are underway to divert water from the Yangzi northwards, linking up with similar projects on the Huai River, which will eventually irrigate the large arid areas of north China.

Neolithic rice-growing cultures occupied this area as early as 5000 BC, domesticating pigs and dogs. By the fifth century BC much of the lower Yangzi formed one of nine huge provincial areas known as Yangzhou; its imperial tribute included silks, fruits and timber. During the Tang Dynasty (618–907) the city of Yangzhou was the main port of call for Arabian traders.

The town of Jiangyin demarcates the estuary, and for the next 200 kilometres (125 miles) the Yangzi widens from 1,200 metres (1,300 yards) to 91 kilometres (56 miles) below the confluence with the Huangpu, the last of its tributaries. In ancient times the Yangzi was said to have had three mouths; down the centuries the river outlet was a source of much academic speculation in China, as silt deposits continually changed the shape and form of the river's mouth. Now its outlet to the Yellow Sea is divided into two by the intensely cultivated island of Chongming (1,083 square kilometres, or 420 square miles, in area) and by several smaller islands, whose farming produce supplies the massive Shanghai area.

In August 1983, when low-lying land in 30 Anhui counties which border the Yangzi was inundated by flood waters, nearly a million peasants battled to drain the land and sow autumn crops. Ninety people were reported dead and hundreds injured as the flood crest swept by. In Jiangsu, 500,000 civilians and soldiers reinforced dikes and stood watch as floods threatened Nanjing and other cities along the banks. Luckily no further serious damage occurred.

## Xiaogu Shan

About 35 kilometres (22 miles) below the mouth of the Boyang, the magical little island of Xiaogu Shan comes into view. It is situated by the north bank of the Yangzi in Anhui Province, while across the river is the county town of Pengze in Jiangxi.

The white walls and grey tiled roofs of Qisu Monastery nestle into Xiaogu Shan's steep slope, and pavilions adorn its bamboo-groved peak. Six elderly monks inhabit the temple (first established in the Song Dynasty), which is dedicated to Xiaogu Niang Niang, and visited by childless women offering incense to her.

As a result of silt accumulation, Xiaogu Shan now adjoins the riverbank. The characters 'First Pass of the Sea Gate' are painted on the rock face. Stairs lead up to the monastery, but to reach the peak one must cling to chains fixed to the rock to negotiate the steep climb.

The island is named after the legendary Lin Xiaogu, later known as Xiaogu Niang Niang, who grew up in Fujian Province and became betrothed to a local village lad, Peng Liang. Unhappily, her parents died, and she was adopted by a Daoist Immortal at Mount Emei in Sichuan Province, where she studied Daoism for many years. One day, while gathering herbs on the mountain, she slipped and fell, and was saved by a wandering woodcutter who was none other than Peng Liang. Peng's mother, attending to the girl's injuries, noticed a small birthmark behind her ear and recognized her as the long-lost Lin Xiaogu. In renewing her betrothal to Peng Liang, Xiaogu broke her religious vows and was incarcerated by the Immortal.

With the help of a sympathetic monk she stole the Immortal's precious umbrella, and the lovers flew away. However, the pursuing Immortal cut off their escape at Boyang Lake with his flying sword, which tore the umbrella and caused Xiaogu to drop her slipper (see page 110). At Pengze the umbrella finally split in two. The lovers fell on different sides of the Yangzi, turning into two steep hills: Pengliang Ji on the south and Xiaogu Shan on the north. The temple on Pengliang Ji was destroyed in the Cultural Revolution.

At the top of Xiaogu Shan is her 'Makeup and Dressing Terrace'. A stone tablet beside it describes her story, as well as a related anecdote concerning Zhu Yuanzhong, founder of the Ming Dynasty, who was apparently saved by the appearance of Xiaogu Niang Niang while retreating downstream one night after a naval defeat.

About 32 kilometres (20 miles) below Pengze the river enters Anhui and winds its way northeast across the province until, just below Maanshan, it enters the province of Jiangsu. Bulk carriers, strings of barges and fishing sampans — their nets attached to long bamboo poles extending forward and aft — frequent the stretch of river between here and Anqing, about three hours' sailing downriver. The south bank is hilly while the north bank is flat, broken only by trees and bamboo groves. A number of shallow lakes feed into the river.

## Anqing

The city of Anqing, on the north bank, is situated in that area of Anhui Province called Huainan, meaning south of the Huai River. It is built along the Dalong Hills amidst pretty surroundings. Historical records refer to the appointment of an official to the town as early as the Spring and Autumn period. During the Qing Dynasty (1644–1911) and the Republican period (1911–49) the city was the capital of the province, though today the capital is Hefei, further north. Anqing's main function is to gather and distribute local produce; it also has a petrochemical industry.

The handsome octagonal **Zhenfeng Pagoda**, the major landmark, was built in 1570 amidst the remains of the Song-Dynasty Welcoming the River Temple (Yingjiang Si). A fine view of the city can be enjoyed from its top storey.

The pagoda was built by a Daoist architect, Zhang Wencai, who was brought to Anqing specially from Baiyun Temple in Beijing. Stone balconies surround six of its seven storeys. Inside, over 600 Buddha images cover the brick walls. Set into the lower half of the pagoda are images of the local prefect, Wang Erquan, who commissioned its construction, and other personages of the period.

The town was occupied by the Taiping rebels for six years and one of its 'kings' built a residence here. It seems that the imperial defences of Anqing left much to be desired, for when it fell to the rebels in 1853 Emperor Xianfeng memorialized: 'Great has been my indignation on reading the memorial . . . how could that important provincial capital be captured by the bandits in one day?' The city, retaken in 1861, was ravaged. Travellers to the city 60 years later noted that large parts of it were still in ruins.

Riverboats stop at **Guichi** (at the mouth of the Qiupu River), which is the closest Yangzi port for those visiting the sacred Buddhist mountain of Jiuhua and the famous scenic area of Huangshan to the south. Though transport facilities to these sites are being developed at Guichi, the city of Wuhu, further downriver, offers more.

## Wuhu

Wuhu, on the south bank of the river, is in southeastern Anhui Province at the confluence of the Qingyi and Yangzi Rivers. Its population is only 440,000, not large by Chinese standards. In the last century Wuhu was one of the four great rice marketing centres (the others being Wuxi, Jiujiang and Changsha), but it is now principally a producer of light industrial goods, such as thermos flasks, machine

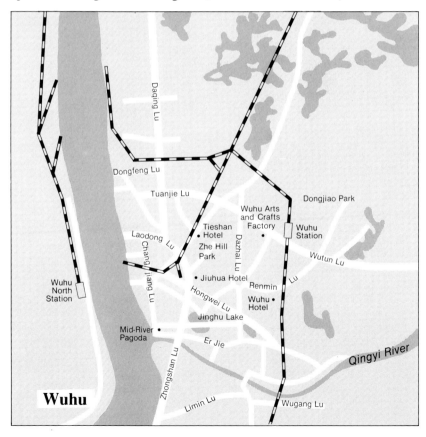

tools, cotton textiles, kitschy mantlepiece clocks, and cement. It is specially known for its scissors, its variety of local twig and leaf brooms and its wrought-iron pictures.

As a good transportation system links Wuhu with other parts of the province, the city is a transfer stop for visitors to the famous scenic spots of Huangshan and Jiuhua.

## History of Wuhu

In the Spring and Autumn period (770−476 BC) the city was known as Jiuzi. Its present name was adopted in the Han Dynasty (206 BC−AD 220). By the Three Kingdoms period (220−65) it had become a strategically important town in the Kingdom of Eastern Wu. In a fierce battle between the Kingdoms of Eastern Wu and Shu, the Wu general Zhou Yu was killed. The King of Wu, Sun Quan, donned white mourning clothes and made a special journey to Wuhu to receive Zhou Yu's coffin. In the Tang Dynasty (618−907) the poet Du Fu's many visits were recollected in his poem, *Thoughts on Staying Again at · Wuhu*. When Wuhu became a Treaty Port under the Chefoo Convention of 1876 a small foreign community resided here. Trading principally in rice, wood and tea, it had become a flourishing commercial port by the end of the 19th century. Trade dropped off severely in the 1920s and '30s due to bandit activity in the area.

## What to See in Wuhu

There is little of historical interest to be found in Wuhu, but a stroll along the east embankment of the Qingyi River is worthwhile. Here barges and small boats load and discharge vegetables, fruit, sand and everyday items; boat families and their pets add to the cacophony of noise. Bamboo rafts, at intervals along the river's edge, serve as platforms for the local women doing their washing. In the narrow streets parallel to the river, such as Zhongchang Jie and Shangchang Jie, shops sell fishing tackle and nets, baskets, firecrackers, bamboo steamers, and Chinese weights and measures. In the cobbled streets, bamboo chicken coops stand outside front doors that open into dark, high-ceilinged old houses. Xinwu Jie running west off the main street, Zhongshan Jie, is busy with restaurants and food stalls serving crispy rice cakes, sweet dumpling soup and large dough fritters. Near the scruffy memorial to the 1949 Revolution is Jiuhe Jie, which is now a market area. At No. 26 a huge, fanciful, American-built Catholic Church, dating from the Treaty Port days, is open for worship on Sundays. At Jinghu Lake, in the town centre, people gather to play cards or chess and to sell their miniature potted plants.

## Zhe Hill

The highest point in the city is only 86 metres (282 feet), but the view from the pagoda at the top sweeps over the whole city and down the Yangzi. It seems that this five-storey **Zheshan Pagoda** and the Mid-River Pagoda (see below) were built at the same time, at the beginning of the Song Dynasty. A competition apparently developed between the two teams of builders. The two brothers engaged on the construction of Zheshan Pagoda, who were desperate to complete first and so avoid losing face, finished off the very top with a cooking 'wok' turned upside down. A small zoo is to be found in the public park.

## Guangji Temple

Of the four main temples which existed in Wuhu, three were destroyed in the Sino-Japanese War and only the Guangji Temple, at the foot of Zhe Hill, remains. The main hall is hung with ten scrolls depicting the Buddhist Hell. The monastery was established in the Tang Dynasty (618–907) and Emperor Dezong (reigned 780–5) came here as a monk. When omens indicated that this was an unsafe place for him to reside, he went to live on the famous Buddhist mountain of Jiuhua, further south.

## Mid-River Pagoda

This six-storey pagoda stands at the point where the Qingyi River enters the Yangzi, a danger spot for navigation. A local fisherman named Huang suggested that this octagonal pagoda be built to serve as a lighthouse. Its name derives from its position — it is exactly in the middle of the lower reaches of the Yangzi.

## Wuhu Arts and Crafts Factory

The art of wrought-iron picture-making originated in Wuhu and this factory in Jiuhua Lu continues the tradition, besides producing pictures made of feathers or golden wheat stalks, poker-burned wooden decorations and copies of old paintings.

Iron picture-making is very laborious and amazingly intricate. This art form was started by an itinerant blacksmith, Tang Tianchi, during the reign (1662–1723) of Emperor Kangxi. Tang used to sit and watch a local painter, whose work he much admired. The artist chided Tang: 'I paint my pictures, you beat your iron, but you will never make pictures by beating iron.' Tang promptly went away and produced an iron picture, 'using a hammer as a brush and iron as ink'.

A huge 'Welcoming Pine' iron picture by the artists of Wuhu adorns the Anhui Room in the Great Hall of the People in Beijing.

## Maanshan

Anhui's biggest industrial city, Maanshan mines much of the pig iron used in the Shanghai steel industry. It also has its own iron and steel works, limestone quarries, and chemical and cement factories. The city is linked to Wuhu and Nanjing by rail.

A touching story is told of the city's name, which means Horse Saddle Hill. When the Kingdoms of Chu and Shu were at war in the third century, General Xiang Yu of Chu was defeated by Liu Bei and attempted to retreat to Wujiang on the north bank of the Yangzi. Finding only a small boat, he had his precious mount ferried across first. At this moment Liu Bei's pursuing soldiers arrived and Xiang Yu, knowing he was trapped, cut his throat with his own sword. Seeing his master's courageous suicide, the horse leapt into the river and drowned. The boatman buried its saddle on the nearby hill.

Buildings on **Coloured Stone Cliff (Caishi Ji)**, west of the city, commemorate the Tang poet Li Bai (701−62). The three-storeyed Taibai Lou houses two Chinese boxwood statues of the poet, one depicting his immortal gesture of inviting the moon to join him in a cup of wine. Here too is the 'Tomb of Li Bai's Clothes and Official Hat'. According to the local legend, Li Bai's clothing was buried on Caishi Ji when he drowned after falling drunkenly from a boat one evening while attempting to embrace the moon's reflection in the river.

The Three Scholars Grotto (Sanyuan Dong) was allegedly built by three grateful scholars. These gentlemen, on their way to the capital to take the imperial examinations, found safety and shelter under the cliff when their boat was caught in a sudden and violent storm. After all three had gained first-class honours and promotions, they recalled their close shave and donated funds for the building of this grotto.

## Nanjing

Nanjing — 'Southern Capital' — along with Luoyang, Xi'an and Beijing, is one of the historical capitals of China, and the many imperial tombs and architectural remains in the city and its environs reflect its grandiose past. Today, the city is the capital of Jiangsu Province, with a population of some 4.5 million. Its industries include machine-building, automobile assembly, electronics, petroleum, iron and steel, textiles, shipbuilding and foodstuffs. A double tiered road and rail bridge, completed in 1968, spans the Yangzi at Nanjing.

### History of Nanjing

With the Yangzi on one side, and surrounded on the other three sides by hills, Nanjing was thought to be auspicious as well as strategically important. First historical records date from the Spring and Autumn period (770−476 BC) when the area was divided between the Kingdoms of Wu, Yue and Chu. A walled town was built during the Eastern Han period (25−220), known as 'Stone City'.

Between the third and 14th centuries, eight dynasties established their capitals in the city, some of them building magnificent palaces and forts. Though many of these minor dynasties had incompetent rulers and regimes weakened by intrigue and debauchery, Nanjing emerged as a cultural centre of painting, philosophy and Buddhism. In the sixth century, the Sui Dynasty established its capital at Xi'an, and ordered the complete destruction of earlier dynastic buildings in Nanjing.

The city flourished again during the Tang Dynasty (618−907), when the great poets Li Bai, Bai Juyi and Liu Yuxi lived here for a while. For a brief period, Nanjing (then called Jinling) became the capital of the Southern Song, but the dynastic base had to be moved to Hangzhou as the pursuing Nuzhen Tartar armies advanced. Marco Polo visited the city in 1275.

The founder of the Ming Dynasty, Zhu Yuanzhang, captured Nanjing in 1356 and set up his capital here, building palaces, temples and pagodas. (The famous green and white glazed-tiled Porcelain Pagoda of the Baoen Temple, so often praised as one of the seven wonders of the world by earlier travellers, belonged to this period, though it was totally destroyed during the Taiping Rebellion. Some of its tiles are on exhibition at the Chaotian Gong.) He also enlarged the city wall to make it the longest in the world. Earlier Tang poets had written lyrically of being entertained on 'singsong boats' — a sort of floating bordello — along the Qinhuai (a ten-kilometre, or six-mile man-made river, said to have been dug during the second century BC, skirting the western and southern edges of Nanjing). A picture of more innocent pleasures is conjured up by a passage from *The Scholars*, an early 18th-century novel by Wu Ching-tzu:

After the middle of the fourth month in Nanking, the Chin-huai River becomes quite lovely. The barges from other tributaries of the Yangtze dismantle their cabins, set up awnings, and paddle into the river. Each vessel carries a small, square, gilt-lacquered table, set with an Yihsing stoneware pot, cups of the finest Cheng Hua or Hsuan Te porcelain, and the choicest tea brewed with rain water. Boating parties bring wine, dishes and sweetmeats with them to the canal, and even people travelling by boat order a few cents' worth of good tea to drink on board as they proceed slowly on their way. At dusk two bright horn lanterns on each vessel are reflected in the water as the barges ply to and fro, so that above and below are bright. Fluting and singing are heard all night and every night from Literary Virtue Bridge to Lucky Crossing Bridge and East Water Guardhouse. The pleasure-goers buy water-

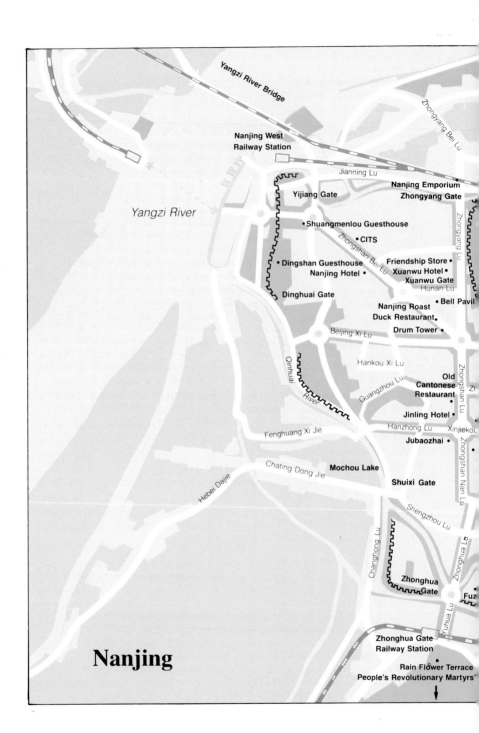

Yangzi River Bridge

Nanjing West
Railway Station

Jianning Lu

Nanjing Emporium

Yijiang Gate

Zhongyang Gate

Yangzi River

• Shuangmenlou Guesthouse

• CITS

Friendship Store •

• Dingshan Guesthouse

Xuanwu Hotel •

Nanjing Hotel •

Xuanwu Gate

Hunan Lu

Dinghuai Gate

• Bell Pavil

Nanjing Roast
Duck Restaurant •

Beijing Xi Lu

Drum Tower •

Hankou Xi Lu

Qinhuai

Old
Cantonese
Restaurant

Guangzhou Lu

River

Jinling Hotel •

Fenghuang Xi Jie

Hanzhong Lu

Xinjiekou

Jubaozhai •

Chating Dong Jie

Mochou Lake

Hebei Dajie

Shuixi Gate

Shengzhou Lu

Changhong Lu

Zhonghua
Gate

Fuz

Zhonghua Gate
Railway Station

Rain Flower Terrace •
People's Revolutionary Martyrs'

Nanjing

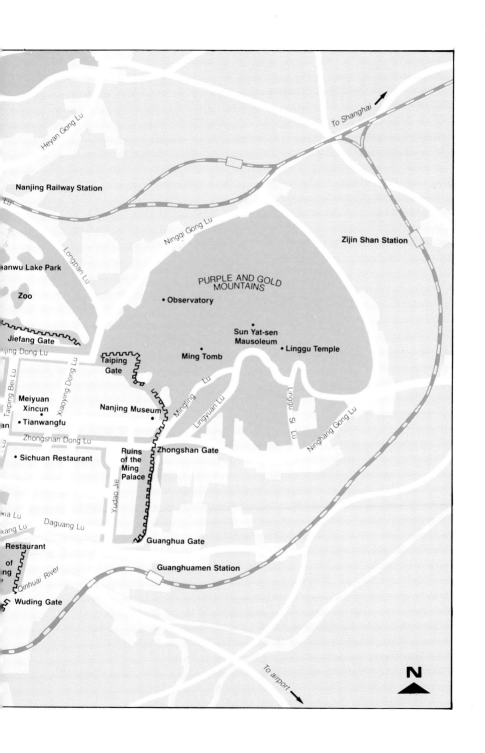

Heyan Gong Lu

To Shanghai

Nanjing Railway Station

Ningqi Gong Lu

Zijin Shan Station

Lu

Longpan Lu

anwu Lake Park

PURPLE AND GOLD
MOUNTAINS

Zoo

• Observatory

Jiefang Gate

Sun Yat-sen
Mausoleum

• Linggu Temple

jing Dong Lu

Taiping
Gate

• Ming Tomb

Xiaoying Dong Lu

Taiping Bei Lu

Mingling Lu

Lingyuan Lu

Linggu Si Lu

Ninghang Gong Lu

Meiyuan
Xincun

Nanjing Museum

an

• Tianwangfu

Zhongshan Dong Lu

Zhongshan Gate

• Sichuan Restaurant

Ruins
of the
Ming
Palace

Yudao Jie

xia Lu

Daguang Lu

ang Lu

Guanghua Gate

Restaurant
of
ng

Guanghuamen Station

Qinhuai River

Wuding Gate

To airport

N

rat fireworks too, which project from the water and look like pear trees in blossom when let off. The fun goes on till the fourth watch each night.

Translated by Yang Hsien-yi and Gladys Yang

During the Ming Dynasty, an imperial decree established a special government department to oversee brothels which catered to the 200,000 garrisoned troops in the city. The capital was moved to Beijing in 1420, but Nanjing remained a subsidiary capital and financial centre.

In the Qing Dynasty (1644–1911) troops were garrisoned in the city. The Treaty of Nanking ending the Opium War of 1842 was signed aboard HMS *Cornwallis* between the British and the Chinese. It ceded the territory of Hong Kong to Britain, opened four Chinese ports to foreign trade, and exacted the payment of 21 million Mexican dollars, as indemnity from the Chinese. It was the first of what became known as the Unequal Treaties. The pseudo-Christian Taiping Rebellion made its headquarters in Nanjing in 1853 and occupied it for 13 years. Its leader, Hong Xiuquan, adopted the title 'Heavenly King' and appointed other leaders as the Princes of the East, West, North and South. The 'Heavenly King' built a palace of thousands of rooms of which little now remains. The city was almost completely destroyed in the devastation and killings which followed the overthrow of this rebellion. Nanjing became a Treaty Port under the terms of the Franco-Chinese Treaty of 1897.

Following the revolution of 1911, Nanjing was declared the capital of the Republic of China in 1912. (Dr Sun Yatsen, founder of the Nationalist Republic, was buried here in 1929.) The Nationalists regained control over Nanjing from the local warlord in 1926, and it remained the capital until just before the Japanese occupation of the city in 1937, when an estimated 400,000 residents perished in what became known as the 'Rape of Nanjing'. In early 1949 the People's Liberation Army entered Nanjing, driving the Nationalist government before it, first to Canton and then to Taiwan.

## What to See in Nanjing

Nanjing's streets are lined with poplars and sycamore trees — some of them brought from France — which provide some relief from the oppressive summer temperatures. Gardens and parks add grace and a sense of spaciousness to the city. Two lakes, **Xuanwu Lake** and **Mochou Lake**, are surrounded by parkland. Many of the historical relics — tombs, steles and sculptures dating from the sixth century on — are to be found in the hills and fields around Nanjing, the best-known in the vicinity of Zijinshan (Purple and Gold Mountain).

## Sights within the City Walls

### Ming-Dynasty City Wall

Built by the first Ming emperor, Hongwu, this wall of clay bricks took 20 years to construct (1366–86), and included remains of an earlier Eastern Han city wall (Stone City). It encloses an area of 41 square kilometres (16 square miles), making it the longest city wall in the world. At its highest point it is 18 metres (60 feet) high, and it varies in width from seven to 12 metres (30 to 40 feet). Some 200,000 workers cemented the bricks — each stamped with details of the brickmaker and overseer — with a mortar mixture of rice gruel paste and lime. The impressive **Zhonghuamen Gate** in the southern part of the city has four vaulted gates and was probably garrisoned by troops; along with the **Hepingmen Gate** these are all that remain of 13 original Ming gates which were largely destroyed in the Taiping Rebellion. Other gates have been built in the 20th century to facilitate traffic flow.

### Ming Bell and Drum Towers  Zhongshan Lu

The Drum Tower marks the centre of Nanjing. It was built in 1382, and was followed in 1388 by the Bell Tower, to the northeast. Both were used to sound out the two-hourly night watches over the city. A tea-room in the Qing-Dynasty pavilion atop the Drum Tower offers a fine view of the city. The Bell Tower houses a one-ton Ming bell. The existing two-storeyed pavilion dates from 1889.

### Jiangsu Provincial Museum  Zhongshanmen Lu

In the six rooms, exhibits include jade, pottery and stone implements from Jiangsu's prehistoric period; artifacts from the Longshan and associated cultures from 4000 to 2500 BC; and a wide range of porcelain, paintings, and bronzes, as well as maps and displays of traditional handicrafts. The famous jade burial suit, exhibited abroad in the 1970s, is a possession of this museum.

Nearby, on Yudao Jie, are the ruined Wumen Gate and Five Dragon Bridges — all that remain of the once-magnificent **Ming Imperial Palace** on which the Imperial Palace of Beijing was modelled.

### Museum of the Taiping Rebellion  Zhanyuan Lu

Housed in the remains of the former palace of the Eastern Prince of the Heavenly Kingdom is the exhibition of maps, paintings, documents and other relics of the Taiping Rebellion. Many of the documents are copies, as the originals are held in Beijing. Beside it is the Zhan Yuan, a traditional Chinese garden which originated in the early Ming Dynasty and eventually became incorporated into the palace of the Eastern Prince, Yang Xiuqing, in the 19th century.

**Zhou Enlai's Delegation House**  30 Meiyuanxincun
At the end of the Sino-Japanese War, abortive peace talks took place
between the Guomindang and the Communist Party of China. During
this period — May 1946 to March 1947 — the late Premier Zhou Enlai
took up residence at 30 Meiyuanxincun. Another revolutionary, Dong
Biwu, resided at No. 35, while their headquarters was at No. 17. These
buildings are now museums to that period.

**Ming Examination Hall**  Gongyuan Jie
Imperial examinations were held at the capital every three years during
the early Ming Dynasty; even when the capital was moved to Beijing,
candidates for high office travelled to Nanjing from nearby provinces.
The Examination Hall comprised 20,600 tiny cubicles in which
candidates were locked and kept guarded during the three-day
examinations. Food was passed in daily to sustain the candidates
through the trying ordeal. A stone bridge and a square tower are all
that remain of this huge establishment. Inside the tower are steles
inscribed with the rules of conduct for the examinations and the history
of the hall itself.

**Fuzi Miao**
In the south of the city, near a stretch of the Qinhuai River, is a newly
developed area where Qing-style buildings house shops and
restaurants. The city fathers are recreating the bustling bazaar that
clustered round the Song-Dynasty Confucius Temple (Fuzi Miao)
which stood here. The temple, destroyed by the Japanese in the 1940s,
has been reconstructed. Fuzi Miao is in Gongyuan Jie, off Jiankang
Lu.

**Site of the Palace of the Heavenly King**  Changjiang Lu
Xuyuan Garden, a lake, and a large stone boat are all that remain of
the large palace built by Hong Xiuquan (1813—64), instigator of the
Taiping Rebellion and self-styled 'Heavenly King'. His palace was
destroyed by the Qing troops at the defeat of the rebellion in 1864.
Local Qing officials used the site as a *yamen* (offices). Later the
Guomindang government buildings were erected on the site. These
were the country's administrative headquarters between 1927 and 1937
(when the Japanese entered the city). The late Generalissimo Chiang
Kai-shek's office was in this complex during that period. Today the
Nanjing Municipal Party Committee occupies the buildings. Foreigners
may only visit with a Public Security Bureau permit.

**Jimingsi (Cock Crow Temple)**  Beijige Hill
The halls date from the late Qing Dynasty, but house Ming sculpture.
Since it was believed that the ghosts of those killed on this site — a

Yuan-Dynasty execution ground — needed appeasement, the first Ming emperor, Hongwu, decreed the construction of this temple. It was a nunnery until the Cultural Revolution.

## Sight outside the City Walls

### Yuhuatai (Terrace of the Rain of Flowers)

A monument to 100,000 Communist revolutionaries killed on this site — used by the Guomindang as an execution ground — was erected in 1950. In the sixth century, the legend goes, a Buddhist monk, Yun Guang, lived and preached here. So eloquent was he that the heavens showered flowers upon him, and these turned into beautiful little agate stones. These rain-flower pebbles are sold to visitors in containers of water to enhance their coloration.

## Sights on Zijinshan (Purple and Gold Mountain)

The three peaks of **Zijinshan** (the highest, 448 metres, or 1,470 feet) form this evergreen scenic area east of Nanjing. Some of the city's most famous sights are to be seen here.

### Mingxiaoling (Tomb of the Ming Emperor)

The first emperor of the Ming Dynasty, Hongwu, was buried here in 1398, alongside his empress, Ma Hou, who died in 1382. The tomb, begun in 1381, is recorded as having taken convict labourers three years to complete. Most of the buildings of the mausoleum have been destroyed. The tomb is in poor condition compared to those of Hongwu's descendants, who were buried outside Beijing after the capital was moved there, and the underground vault has yet to be excavated. Remains of a cobbled path lead to the 'spirit way' — the avenue of carved stone animals, warriors and officials. The style of carving — bold and simple — is typical of the early Ming period. The animals represented (including the mythical *qilin* and *xiezhi*) are in two pairs, one pair standing, the other sitting.

### Dr Sun Yatsen's Mausoleum

Nanjing's most famous landmark is the elegant blue and white mausoleum of Dr Sun Yatsen (1866–1925), father of the Chinese Republic. Dr Sun's body was kept at the Biyun Monastery in the Western Hills of Beijing until this mausoleum was completed in 1929. 'Universal Love' are the characters above the triple-arched gateway, through which an avenue of tall trees leads to the main gate, with 'The world belongs to everyone' in Chinese emblazoned on it. A flight of 392 marble steps leads to the memorial hall in which is a seated,

gypsum statue of Dr Sun (sculpted in France by a Polish friend,
Landowski). Dr Sun's remains are beneath a recumbent marble statue
of him (executed by Japanese associates) in the circular crypt behind
the hall. The mausoleum was designed by Lu Yanzhi and the colours
are those of the Guomindang flag. The mausoleum covers 130 square
kilometres (50 square miles).

### Linggu Monastery
In order to build his grand mausoleum on an auspicious site, the Ming
emperor Hongwu had first to remove an existing temple, the Linggusi,
to its present wooded peak. All that remains of that Ming temple is the
46-metre (150-foot) long **Beamless Hall (Wuliang Dian)**, made of brick
with no supporting wooden beams. A handsome *pailou* or gateway
leads to the hall. West of the hall is the flat **Coiled Dragons Stone**,
found beside a nearby pool, on which monks once meditated. The
nine-storeyed **Linggu Pagoda** was built in the 1930s. The present
Linggu Monastery, to the southeast, dates from the late Qing period
and is occupied by a community of monks.

### Zijinshan Observatory
Situated on one peak of Zijinshan, this third largest of China's
observatories was built in 1934. Reproductions of Han- and Yuan-
period astrological instruments — celestial globe, armillary sphere,
seismograph, theodolite, clepsydra and ancient sundial — are on
display.

## Sights on Qixia Mountain

Seventeen kilometres (10.5 miles) east of Nanjing, the drive to the
Buddhist grottoes and temple of Qixia takes the visitor through an area
rich in tomb sites of the nobility of the Liang Dynasty (502–57). In
particular there are stone figures from the tombs of three of Emperor
Wudi's brothers, Xiao Dan, Xiao Hui and Xiao Xiu. Xiao Dan's tomb
includes a well-preserved stele on the back of a stone tortoise and two
large stone winged lions. Xiao Xiu's tomb figures include wonderfully
carved winged lions, tortoises and columns.

### Qixia Monastery
First built in the fifth century, this monastery has been destroyed and
restored repeatedly thereafter. The monastery's abbot trains Buddhist
monks, under the auspices of the Chinese Buddhist Theological
Institute. The monastery has a valuable library. Behind the monastery
is the **Sheli Pagoda**, one of the oldest stone pagodas south of the
Yangzi River. This 15-metre (50-foot) high, five-storeyed pagoda was
built in 601, and is embellished with detailed carvings of Buddha's life.

**Qixia Buddhist Grottoes**
There are more than 500 statues in nearly 300 grottoes in the vicinity of
the monastery. The earliest date from the fifth century, and they
continued to be carved until the Ming Dynasty. One figure is a 13-
metre (43-foot) high Buddha, said to have been carved by
Zhongzhang, son of the magistrate-turned-hermit, Ming Sengshao
(who donated his home as the original Qixia Monastery).

# Zhenjiang

Zhenjiang, on the south bank, with a population of 390,000, is situated
in the middle of Jiangsu Province, at the junction of the Yangzi and
the Grand Canal, 63 kilometres (40 miles) from Nanjing. It was the
capital of the province during the Republican period (1911−49) when
Nanjing was the national capital. Earlier Chinese travellers classified
Zhenjiang's scenery as 'The Best Landscape under Heaven', and

indeed the area known as the Southern Suburbs was often used as a theme in landscapes by famous Chinese painters. Marco Polo visited the city in the 13th century, commenting: 'The people of Zhenjiang live by industry and commerce; they produce much silk and brocade and the rustic flavour of the place is suitable for the production of many things.'

The American Nobel Prize-winning writer, Pearl Buck (1892–1973), author of *The Good Earth* and other novels about China, lived in Zhenjiang for 15 years before attending boarding school in Shanghai. Her missionary parents' house still stands in the northern part of the city, incorporated into a radio factory.

Handicrafts include jade carvings, palace lanterns and screens of natural stone. Zhenjiang is also known for its black vinegar and pickled vegetables.

## History of Zhenjiang

Zhenjiang, under various names, has existed for 2,500 years. In 213 BC, its importance as a ferry crossing led Emperor Qin Shihuangdi to conclude that Zhenjiang's *fengshui* (geomantic) powers were too strong. He ordered 3,000 prisoners to dig a tunnel through one of the hills to divert the influences. During the convoluted politics of the Three Kingdoms period (220–65) Zhenjiang was the site of many 'mini-summits' on military strategy between the warring kingdoms.

Tens of thousands of soldiers clashed in a battle between imperial forces and a peasant army during the Eastern Jin (317–419). Under the Song Dynasty (960–1279) the city's development reached its height, producing fine silks, satins and silverware as tribute to the imperial court. Troops were stationed here to defend the river ('Zhenjiang' means Guard the River) — a wise precaution, as it turned out, when they had to take on invading Jin troops in a naval battle near Jin Shan in 1130.

The city played its part in the shipment of grain, salt and other merchandise along the Grand Canal until the early part of the 20th century, when railways displaced river transport.

During the Opium War of 1842, Zhenjiang was bombarded by British men-of-war. Seven thousand British troops stormed the walled city, which was defended by only about 3,000 courageous Chinese soldiers. The governor of the city and his family committed suicide. On the British side, 105 soldiers were killed or wounded. This battle was a turning point, as it led to the signing of the Treaty of Nanking only a month later. This treaty provided for the surrender of Hong Kong to Britain and for the payment of 21 million Mexican dollars by the Chinese as indemnity.

The city was again captured in 1853 by the Taiping rebels and held by them for four years, which left it crippled. A small foreign concession area was established in 1861. A.H. Rasmussen, a Scandinavian trader who lived in Zhenjiang for many years, wrote:

... Then I went into the silent street for a breath of fresh air and walked up and down the bund, three hundred paces one way and three hundred paces back. To get a little change I walked up and down the only cross street to the south gate of the Concession, two hundred paces one way and two hundred paces back.

Life was very restricted, and the hunting of wild boar in the surrounding hills became the main pastime for the resident foreigners.

## What to See in Zhenjiang

The busiest area of the city is within the confines of Zhengdong Lu, Jiefang Lu and Renmin Lu. The old city is further west, near Boxian Park. The foreign concession was there; its British consulate is now the **Zhenjiang Museum**. On Boxian Lu an old American church still retains the stone plaque set into a wall which reads, though not clearly:

First Baptist Church
Organized
.......... D 1885
Rebuilt 1921

### Xiao Matou Jie (Small Jetty Street)

Take this charming little cobbled street through the oldest part of town. The rows of Qing-Dynasty buildings are intersected by stone arches at regular intervals. One of these is the **Zhaoguan Dagoba** — five metres (16 feet) high above a stone archway — which dates from the Yuan Dynasty. The names engraved on either side commemorate those who were officials of the prefecture when the dagoba was restored in 1583. The cobbled pathway was once lined with shops selling incense to devotees at Jin Shan Temple. West of the dagoba is the Western Ferry Crossing (Xi Jindu Jie). Its stone steps once led straight down to the riverside, where there was a ferry service to Jin Shan and the other side of the Yangzi. Marco Polo is said to have come ashore at this very spot.

### Jin Shan (Golden Hill)

The 44-metre (144-foot) high Golden Hill, with its famous monastery, was an island in the centre of the Yangzi until it merged with the river bank in the middle of the last century. Visitors used to take a ferry from the Western Ferry Crossing, and then rode mules to the top. Jin

Shan Monastery was first built over 1,500 years ago. In its heyday, the monastery was looked after by 3,000 Buddhist monks.

Visitors may be shown the most interesting of the several sights and relics on Jin Shan. **Jin Shan Pagoda** was first built 1,400 years ago and rebuilt many times: in the Song Dynasty as two pagodas, in the Ming as a single tower and three times in the Qing period. **Fa Hai or Pei Gong Cave** is identified by a statue of the monk Fa Hai, son of a Tang-Dynasty Prime Minister. Fa Hai lived here when he came to the monastery, having first studied at Lushan. It is said that when the monk discovered a pot of gold, he gave it to the local officials. The emperor ordered that the gold be returned to Fai Hai, to rebuild the monastery, thereafter named Golden Hill Monastery.

The extraordinary folktale of the White Snake is connected to Fa Hai. The story tells of a 1,000-year old white snake, Bai Suzhen, who, longing for a life among mortals, changed herself into a beautiful maiden. She married a young herbalist, Xu Xian, whom she first met on the famous Broken Bridge on the West Lake in Hangzhou. The happy couple set up business dispensing medicines, but Suzhen's magical cures aroused the anger of the powerful Buddhist monk Fa Hai. His machinations put the couple through many trials and tribulations before Xu Xian was rescued from his temple prison and Fa Hai defeated. At one point Xu Xian escaped through the **Bai Long Dong (White Dragon Cave)** on Jin Shan, for though narrow it is said to lead to Hangzhou where the herbalist and Suzhen were reunited.

In the monastery, a bronze drum, presented in the Qing Dynasty, is one of the treasures of the **Four Precious Room (Sibao Shi)**. It is believed to have belonged to Zhuge Liang (181–234) and to have doubled as a cooking pot when not being beaten in war. Another is Su Dongpo's official mandarin belt of 20 jade pieces. Su apparently had to forfeit his belt when he lost a debate on Buddhism with his friend, the monk Fo Yin.

The scroll-adorned **Fo Dian (Buddha Hall)**, with its 18 *luohan* (disciples of Buddha) statues, is where the monks hold their services.

West of Jin Shan, along the road that runs beside an artificial lake, is **Zhongling Spring**, the 'Foremost Spring under Heaven'. It was graded by the Tang scholar, Lu Yu, whose *Book of Teas* listed and classified seven springs in China in accordance with the water's compatibility with tea. Zhongling's water was judged the sweetest for brewing tea. The bubbling spring trickles into a small pool enclosed by bamboo groves, but today its water is anything but sweet.

### Beigu Shan

Rising from the Yangzi the steep cliff face of the 53-metre (174-foot) high Beigu Shan was a natural fortification and was chosen by Sun

Quan, King of Wu, as the site of his capital, Tiewangcheng, in the third century. The Martyr's Monument now stands where the great Wu General, Zhou Yu, made his headquarters. The novel *Romance of the Three Kingdoms* contains many stories concerning Beigu Shan.

The exquisite **Iron Pagoda** dates from the Song Dynasty and has an extraordinary history of survival. Erected in the 11th century on the site of an earlier pagoda, it had nine tiers. In the Ming Dynasty, a tidal wave destroyed seven tiers, which were later replaced. In the Qing, the upper tiers were again destroyed, this time by lightning. Several Ming tiers were discovered nearby during restoration in 1961 and replaced in position above the only two remaining original Tang tiers. Over 2,000 Tang relics were also found at that time. The **Ganlu (Sweet Dew) Temple** buildings now house painting exhibits.

The **Hen Stone** was carved into the shape of a ram at the end of the last century. It is believed that the King of Wu sat on this stone when planning his strategy for the great Red Cliff Battle (see page 92).

The pretty **Duojing Lou** is said to have been the dressing room of Liu Bei's wife, the sister of Sun Quan. Song Dynasty literati frequently held banquets in it.

From the **Jijiang Ting (Sacrificing to the River Pavilion)** Liu Bei's wife is said to have committed suicide. She threw herself into the river upon hearing of the death of her husband at Baidi Cheng (see page 58), after his defeat by her brother's army.

The two **Shijian Shi (Sword Testing Stones)**, each split neatly in two, were reputedly cloven by the swords of Liu Bei and Sun Quan, who were at that time outwardly in alliance over regaining the city of Jingzhou (present-day Jiangling, see page 89) but secretly plotting to betray the other.

The three characters *Liu ma jian* — 'Hold back the horse from the cliff' — on the face below the hill, are associated with a story that also involves Liu and Sun. At a banquet together, Liu, who being from the northwest was an expert cavalryman but was less adept at naval warfare, said to Sun, 'Now I know why southerners can row boats so well, and northerners manage their horses.' Sun took offence at what he considered a backhanded compliment, and challenged Liu to a race. In a drunken state they leapt on to their horses. As they reached the cliff edge Liu reined in his horse, but Sun could not and was saved from death only at the last moment by Liu.

### Jiao Shan

Four kilometres (2.5 miles) northeast of Zhenjiang, the tiny island of Jiao Shan can be reached by a local ferry. It was named after a hermit scholar-monk, Jiao Guang of the Eastern Han period (25–220), who is said to have lived in what is known as the **Three Summons Cave**.

Thrice Jiao was invited by the emperor to take an official post, and thrice he refused. He lived to be 120 years old, treating and healing the local fisherfolk.

At the foot of the hill is **Dinghui Monastery (Monastery of Stability and Wisdom)** built on the site of an earlier temple in the Tang Dynasty. It was burnt down and rebuilt in the Ming. Old gingko trees stand in front of the main hall which contains some fine bronze *luohan* (disciples of Buddha) statues, presented by temples at Wutai Shan in Shanxi Province.

The chief attraction of the **Jiao Shan Forest of Tablets**, a collection of over 260 inscribed stones classified into literary, artistic and historic works, the earliest of which date from the Eastern Jin Dynasty, is the White Crane Tablet cut with the calligraphy of Wang Yizhe (321–79). Wang was fond of white cranes (which symbolize longevity) and on seeing one on Jiao Shan asked if he could have it. The monk refused at first, but on learning Wang's identity agreed that he could collect the crane on his next visit. Returning a year later, Wang discovered that the crane had died and had been buried, wrapped in yellow silk, on the hillside. His text of the sad story of the crane was preserved on a tablet on the hill. Later, during an earthquake, part of the inscription broke off and fell into the river. A thousand years later, in 1713, five pieces were recovered *upstream*, and were restored to their rightful place.

The **Cannon Platform** dates from the first Anglo-Chinese Opium War. (Another lies on Elephant Hill on the south bank of the Yangzi.) In the course of the war, British naval ships sailed up the river and, in a two-pronged attack, captured the stronghold, killing 500 Chinese troops. The walls — pock-marked with cannon shell — are made of rammed earth and sticky-rice water.

Near the top of the hill are viewing pavilions and the **Bie Feng Yan** cottage in which Zheng Banqiao (1693–1765), one of the Eight Eccentric Painters of the Yangzhou school, lived for five years.

## Grand Canal

The Grand Canal zigzags some 2,500 kilometres (1,554 miles) down the length of eastern China and remains the longest man-made waterway in the world. In ancient times the canal was crucial in the transportation of grain from the fertile Yangzi delta to the relatively barren north, and in developing communications across the vast territory that the waterway system served. From the Yellow River valley, from which Chinese civilization sprang, culture and learning spread southwards along the canal, until by the Tang Dynasty such cities as Yangzhou and Hangzhou had themselves become centres of art and philosophy.

The first link in this canal system was constructed in the fifth century BC by the King of Wu to facilitate his invasion of the Kingdom of Ji to the north. Other canals were constructed as political and economic demands arose. It was the Sui emperor Yangdi who, in the seventh century, set about creating an inter-communicating system linking the Sui capital of Luoyang with the rice lands of the Yangzi River plains. The network was extended to the northern city, later called Beijing, to supply his armies, then fighting the Koreans. Tens of thousands of men and women were conscripted to labour on these projects, and to plant trees along the banks.

Ma Shumou, the emperor's cruel overseer, was known as Mahu — 'Ma the Barbarous'. Yangzhou mothers to this day chastise their children by threatening 'Mahu will get you'. It was reputed that during the building of the Grand Canal he demanded a daily meal of steamed two-year old child.

During the Tang Dynasty (618–907) over 300,000 tons of grain were shipped northwards annually under the escort of 120,000 soldiers. Yangzhou thrived as the centre for this transshipment trade.

When the Mongol Yuan Dynasty (1279–1368) established its capital in present-day Beijing, the need for a rapid supply of grain, unimpeded by pirates along the sea route, led to the digging of a direct canal northwards, which shortened the route by some 700 to 800 kilometres (435 to 500 miles). The reduced length of 1,782 kilometres (1,108 miles) was bordered by a paved highway allowing travellers to cover the distance in 40 days.

Throughout its history the canal supplied not only the essentials of life but also the luxuries. Scholars and officials travelled on it to and from the capital for imperial examinations or affairs of state. Emperor Yangdi's retinue, in magnificent boats styled as dragons, tigers and birds, was pulled by 80,000 trackers along it.

During the Qing Dynasty (1644–1911) official corruption, flooding and silting caused the gradual decline of the Grand Canal.

Twelve thousand bridges span the canal, which in recent years has been dredged and repaired. Water from the Yangzi is being diverted along this age-old channel for irrigation of the northern plains and the cities of Beijing and Tianjin. Stretches of it are now open to tourism.

## Yangzhou

Yangzhou was one of the most important cities on the Grand Canal and is a delightful place to visit, retaining to some degree the feeling of its rich cultural and historical traditions. A vehicular ferry from Zhenjiang crosses the Yangzi and from the north bank the drive to Yangzhou takes half an hour. Many traditional arts and crafts are still practised: lacquerware, paper-cuts, lanterns, embroidery, *penjing* (miniature gardens) and seal carving. Yangzhou has one of the great cuisines of China and every foreigner knows — indirectly — about it, for Yangzhou is the home of the worldwide favourite Chinese dish of fried rice (*Yangzhou chaofan*).

## History of Yangzhou

The city's history began over 2,400 years ago in the Spring and Autumn period (770—476 BC); one of the early nine provincial areas of China was called after it. The Sui emperor, Yangdi, initiated the construction of the Grand Canal here in 605, which eventually made Yangzhou the hub of land and water transportation. Emperor Yangdi visited the city three times in grand dragon-boats. He built a palace, retired and was buried here, after being assassinated in 618. Yangzhou was also a centre of classical learning and religion. Emperors, prime ministers and men of letters through the ages visited Yangzhou and many held official positions, including the great traveller Marco Polo.

By the Tang Dynasty (618—907), Yangzhou's trading links with Arab merchants were well established. A foreign community numbering about a thousand lived in the city. It was said that 'at night a thousand lanterns lit up the clouds'. The economy was based on the salt monopoly and on grain shipments to the capital.

Yangzhou, along with so many other middle and lower Yangzi cities, suffered badly during the Taiping Rebellion.

During the 17th and 18th centuries an individualistic school of painters sprang up, known as the Eight Eccentrics of Yangzhou, whose bold style has a strong following today.

## What to See in Yangzhou

The streets of Yangzhou reveal much that is charming and interesting. Stroll down Guoqing Jie past craftsmen painting mirrors and making bamboo steamers and cloth shoes, then along Dujiang Lu where wooden-fronted shops, partitioned with rattan matting, sell household goods, basketware and fireworks, and itinerant sugarcane vendors hawk their wares, till the road reaches the Grand Canal, where from the bridge the boat life can be observed as it passes by. The courtyards of the small, grey-tiled houses are cluttered with pots of flowers and miniature *penjing* plants — a speciality of the region. Rows of white cabbage and strips of turnip hang out to dry. One may walk too along the small canals.

The Imperial Jetty, where the Qing emperors disembarked, is situated on the canal in front of Xiyuan Hotel. Visit also **Yechun Yuan** where a poetry club met in the Qing Dynasty. It is now a teahouse and specializes in Yellow Bridge Buns which were first created to supply the troops during the Sino-Japanese War. Further on is the **Luyang Cun**, a garden filled with miniature plants, goldfish and birds.

**Shouxi Lake (Slim West Lake)**
The shores of this lake are scattered with pavilions and halls, many used as tea-rooms. The Fishing Platform at the end of the Dyke of Spring Willows was reputedly used by Emperor Qianlong (reigned 1736—96). Through its arches different views of the beautiful Five-Kiosk Bridge, built in 1757, are presented. The red pillars and yellow-tile roofs of the kiosks rest on 15 stone arches; at the Mid-autumn Festival the moon is said to be reflected in the water under each of them. Emperor Qianlong remarked on a visit that, though this scenic spot reminded him of Beihai Park in Beijing, it was a pity that there was no White Dagoba to complete the resemblance. A copy was

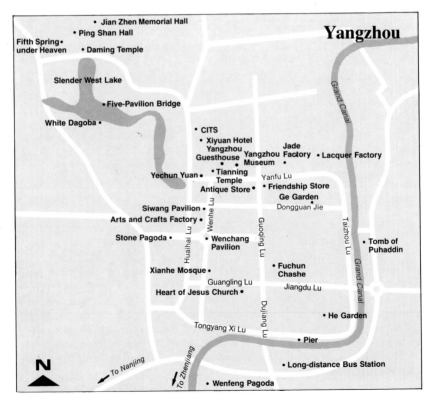

immediately constructed. The Friendship Hall contains a stone tablet with a description of Marco Polo's three-year governorship in Yangzhou, and his portrait. The lovely Yu Garden was built in 1915 as the residence of the local warlord, Yu Baoshan.

### Wenfeng Pagoda

This seven-tiered wooden and brick pagoda stands beside a busy stretch of the Grand Canal south of the city, where boats load and unload goods — bamboo matting, soya beans, rice and cotton. Most of the boats are made of concrete; very few are of wood. Men beating gongs parade up and down with carts; they do the shopping for the boat-people who are too busy to go ashore and do their own.

### Xianhe Temple (Fairy Crane Mosque)

This is one of the four famous old mosques of China (the others are in Guangzhou, Hangzhou and Quanzhou). It was first built in 1275 to serve the needs of the Arab traders and was rebuilt twice in the Ming Dynasty. Its ancient pine and gingko trees are believed to be 800 years old. The mosque is supposed to resemble a crane in shape: the main entrance is the head; the wells on either side, the eyes; the left-hand path, the neck; the prayer hall, the body; the north and south halls, the wings. Arabic scrolls executed in Chinese calligraphic style hang in one of the halls. There are some 3,600 Hui (Moslems) in Yangzhou, but the congregation at Friday prayers is less than 50.

### Tomb of Puhaddin

Puhaddin was a 16th-generation descendant of the Prophet Mohammed, founder of Islam. He came to China in the second half of the 13th century and was in Yangzhou between 1265 and 1275, helping to build the Fairy Crane Mosque. He travelled to Shandong Province to spread the word of Islam, but became ill and died there. He was buried, according to his wish, in Yangzhou.

A fine, carved white marble stairway leads to the cemetery. The majority of the 25 tombs here are those of Chinese Muslims but a few are the tombs of early Arab traders; the architectural style of the tombs is completely Arabian.

### Yangzhou Museum

This building was originally erected in 1772 around the tomb of Shi Kefa (1601–45) who was in command of Yangzhou when the Qing armies moved south to consolidate their power. A supporter of the Ming Dynasty, Shi and his 4,000 troops held out against the Qing army for ten days, five times refusing to surrender and fighting to the death.

The museum displays original works by Yangzhou's Eight Eccentric Painters, as well as stone figures.

## Ge Garden

The delightful garden residence on Dongguan Jie was the home of a rich 19th-century salt merchant, Huang Yingtai. Its architecture, bamboo groves and landscaping are typical of the famous private gardens of Suzhou. The garden got its name from its bamboo leaves, shaped like the Chinese character *ge*. On Xuningmen Jie is the **He Garden**. It once belonged to the Qing Court's ambassador to France, and some Western architectural influences can be discerned.

## Wenchang Pavilion

This 'mini' Temple of Heaven is three storeys high and took ten years to build; just before completion it burnt down, only to be immediately rebuilt in 1585. Originally situated on a bridge across a canal, the area was transformed into a wide roadway, so Wenchang Ge now stands at the intersection of Wenhe Jie and Shita Jie. Nearby is the **Stone Pagoda**, a highly valued Tang-Dynasty relic. Its six sides are decorated with floral patterns.

## Tianning Temple

The present buildings date from the Ming Dynasty, though a temple existed here in the Song Dynasty. The Qing emperor Qianlong had a travel lodge built when on one of his inspection tours. The temple, next to Xiyuan Hotel, was recently restored.

## Daming Temple

Daming Temple is part of a complex of buildings. The temple was built in the fifth century. Large incense burners with bells stand in front of the main hall in which services are held daily at 4 pm.

The temple has strong ties with Japan. The Buddhist abbot Jian Zhen (688–763), invited to teach in Japan, made five attempts to go there, failing each time. It was on his sixth attempt, at the age of 66 and by then blind, that he succeeded in reaching the Japanese capital of Nara where he set up a study centre at one of the temples. His contribution in bringing understanding of Chinese literature and arts, architecture, medicine and printing to Japan was commemorated in 1963, when a number of Chinese and Japanese Buddhists decided to build the **Jian Zhen Memorial Hall**. The walls are decorated with murals depicting his journeys. In 1980 the Japanese donated a copy of a statue of the monk which in Japan is a national treasure.

**Pingshan Hall** was built by the great Song-Dynasty scholar, statesman and poet, Ouyang Xiu, in 1048 to entertain his guests when he was Prefect of Yangzhou. A statue of him now stands in the hall. Su Dongpo, also an official in Yangzhou, wrote a commemorative poem about Ouyang, his teacher, which is engraved in stone on the walls.

In the gardens of the temple is another of the seven great springs of China, mentioned in the Tang-Dynasty *Book of Teas*. This one is known as the 'Fifth Spring under Heaven' (see page 140).

Parts of the Tang city walls can be seen in the vicinity of Daming Temple and on **Guanyin Hill**, the site of the Sui emperor Yangdi's palace.

## Nantong

Nantong is one of the 14 port cities opened to foreign investment projects under China's current policies of modernization. The city is an integral part of the Shanghai Economic Zone. It is hoped that textile, precision machinery and communications industries will be established either as joint ventures or entirely foreign enterprises. Ten thousand-ton vessels berth at its deep-water harbour.

The population of 7.4 million is engaged in industrial production, especially textiles.

One of the city's heroes was Cao Gong, who in 1557 successfully defended the town against Japanese pirates roaming the coast of China. His heroic exploits earned him a high official position which he refused to accept. Cao was killed in another pirate raid shortly after. The **Cao Gong Zhu Memorial Temple** was built in his honour.

East of the city is **Lang Shan** (Wolf Hill), said to be haunted by the spirit of a white wolf. The temple on top is dedicated to a Song-Dynasty Buddhist monk, whom legend endowed with magical powers over water demons. Boat people prayed to him for safe journeys. The main hall contains models of different types of river craft. At the base of Lang Shan is the **Five Hills Park**.

## Baoshan

The giant Baoshan Steel Works on the south bank, near the mouth of the Huangpu River, is planned to be the largest in China. Japanese and West German technology and plant are being used. In the early stages the project ran into difficulties, not the least of which was the choice of site — marshy ground which caused subsidence. Moreover, the estuary was found to be too shallow to allow 100,000-ton freighters bearing imported iron ore to unload. The first phase of the mill began operation in 1985.

# Huangpu River

Just below Baoshan, boats pass by a large lighthouse and between buoys to turn south into the Huangpu River, on the last stage of the journey from Chongqing to Shanghai. The 72-kilometre (44.7-mile) cruise today takes one through the heart of Shanghai's port; on either side of the muddy river stretch wharf installations with facilities to handle oceangoing ships of 25,000 tons and an annual shipping volume of about 100 million tons. This is China's largest port and its busiest. Apart from the hundreds of foreign and Chinese registered ships, the river is busy all day long with ferries, naval and police craft, lighters and dredges.

The Huangpu is 114 kilometres (70 miles) in length, rising from Dianshan Lake southwest of Shanghai. Its banks were once simply mud flats. The river is subject to heavy silting from the Yangzi and requires constant dredging to keep the channels free.

Soon after entering the river, on the western bank is the area known as Wusong, where in 1842, during the Opium War, a fleet of British warships and support vessels opened fire on the ill-defended Chinese fort and its miles of earthworks. After a two-hour bombardment they forced their way up to Suzhou Creek and on to Shanghai. The fort was heroically defended but the Chinese were no match for the British fleet. Among the many Chinese casualties was a highly respected 76-year old admiral who had been at sea for 50 years and who, it was said, wrapped himself in cotton wool before his battles to make himself invulnerable. This was a decisive battle, for it enabled the fleet to occupy Shanghai and move on up the Yangzi; later in the year, the Treaty of Nanking was signed, opening many Chinese cities to foreign trade.

Before the opium trade was legitimized in 1860, opium clippers and steamers unloaded their cargo on to hulks permanently moored at Wusong, Shanghai's outer anchorage for this smuggling.

Gradually Shanghai's imposing skyline appears as boats sidle up to the berth alongside Zhongshan Lu, once known as the Bund, and lined with impressive European-style buildings from a bygone era.

Twin-hulled tourist boats take visitors on a four-hour river trip through Shanghai's docks and up the Huangpu River to the Yangzi. The boats leave from the wharf opposite the Peace Hotel.

## Shanghai

Shanghai is China's second-largest city — it is a conurbation of 13 million people — and is one of three centrally administered cities in the country, the other two being Beijing and Tianjin. It is also one of China's most important industrial and cultural centres.

To most foreigners, Shanghai conjures up stories of adventure and intrigue, of vice and pleasure. Many of these were probably no exaggeration, for it was a dynamic, violent and colourful city. Most of the European-style quarters of the old International Settlement and the French Concession areas can still be seen, though they are much in need of repair. One can still clearly imagine the extraordinary life of pre-1949 Shanghai.

## History of Shanghai

The name Shanghai — 'on the sea' — was first used in AD 960. The settlement was then a backward fishing village. In 1554 the town was· surrounded by a seven-metre (23-foot) high crenellated city wall and a moat to protect it against the frequent incursions of Japanese pirates. By the 17th century there were signs of growing wealth, but when the British troops stormed its undefended walls in 1842, Shanghai was still only a county town of little importance.

The first foreign settlement was established in 1843, when the newly appointed British Consul arrived to negotiate for a 138-acre (just over half a square kilometre) site north of the existing city. The American Settlement, founded in 1848 north of Suzhou Creek, joined with the British to form the International Settlement in 1863. Subsequent negotiations with the Chinese increased the area of the International Settlement to more than 5,500 acres (about 22 square kilometres). The French Concession was established on 164 acres (about 0.6 square kilometres) in 1849 and was finally extended to about 2,500 acres (about ten square kilometres). The Japanese, also, had secured a concession by the end of the last century which became a centre for cotton-spinning factories. These settlements administered themselves and were outside Chinese government jurisdiction.

The old Chinese City, occupied by elements of the Taiping rebels — the Dagger Society — between 1853 and 1855, became the scene of lawlessness and fighting. The foreign community, concerned for its own safety, formed the Shanghai Volunteer Corps, recruited from local traders and diplomats. They were even prepared to take on the imperial troops: backed by British and American officers and men from visiting warships, the volunteers issued an ultimatum for the troops' removal — an action which precipitated the Battle of Muddy Flat in 1854. The imperial troops were duly driven away from their encampment, which was the site of the old racecourse, now the People's Park.

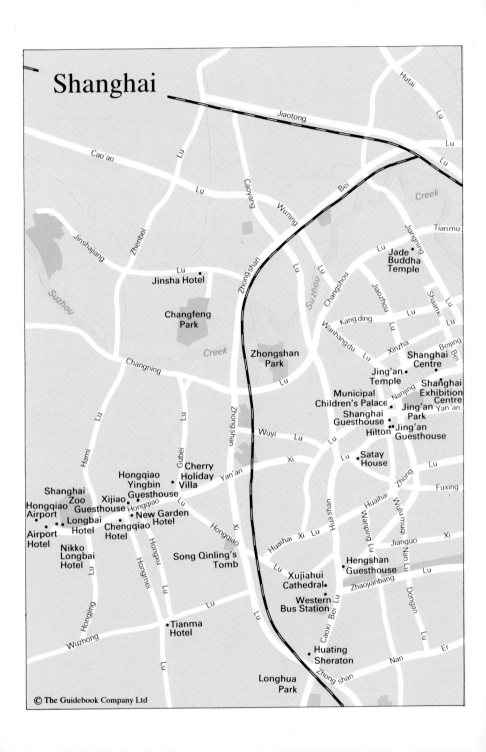

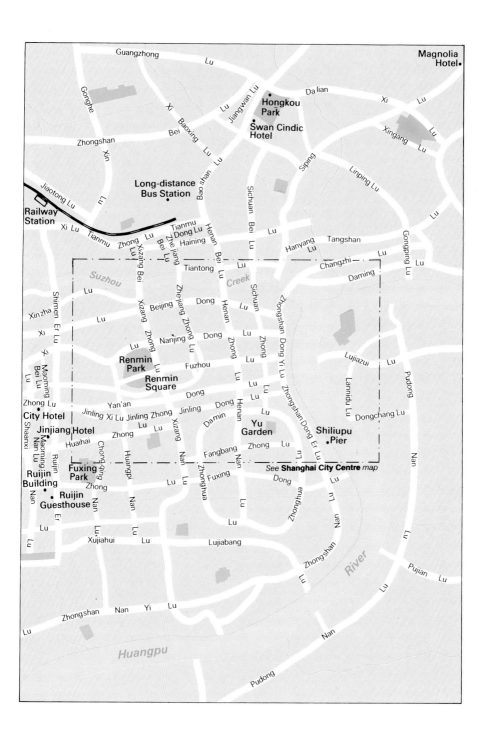

Shanghai was again threatened by the Taiping rebels in the 1860s, but they were quelled by the Ever Victorious Army — made up of foreigners and Chinese — established for this very purpose. An American, Frederick Townsend War, a Frenchman, Henri A. Burgevine, and a Briton, Charles George Gordon ('Chinese Gordon', later of Khartoum fame), took successive command and were all made officers of the Qing imperial army.

The nationwide upheavals in the 20th century — the Boxer Rebellion, the 1911 Revolution, the Sino-Japanese War — took their toll on Shanghai's millions. Hundreds of thousands of Chinese poured into the foreign settlements for protection — and stayed on. Nevertheless, Shanghai continued to flourish as an entrepôt with its staple exports of tea and silk, and imports of piece-goods and opium. Banking played an important part in this great trading city, which had its own stock exchange.

The foreigners' lifestyle was grand and lavish for those who could afford to participate in clubs, race meetings, paper chases and nightclubs. The arrival in the 1930s of some 25,000 White Russian refugees livened the nightlife of cabarets and dance halls in 'Frenchtown', as the French Concession was called by the Anglo-Saxons. Chinese secret societies controlled the seamy side of Shanghai life, and the city was the Hollywood of China with a thriving movie industry.

But the Shanghai workers were subjected to appalling working conditions, overcrowding and exploitation, a situation leading inevitably to industrial unrest and revolutionary activity. The Communist Party of China was founded in Shanghai in 1921, at a secret meeting in the French Concession. The Party fomented strikes and uprisings — some of them actually planned by the late Premier Zhou Enlai — but these activities were violently suppressed by the Nationalist government. This was a period of debate among Chinese intellectuals, who were influenced by the philosophies and experience of the more industrialized West. Many of these Chinese had studied abroad or at missionary institutions of higher learning in Shanghai.

The beginning of the Sino-Japanese War saw bombing and fierce fighting in and around Shanghai, but the foreign concessions were not occupied by the Japanese until after the bombing of Pearl Harbour, when Allied nationals were interned.

In 1945, at the end of the war, the Guomindang government declared an end to all extraterritoriality, so that Shanghai and all the other remaining Treaty Ports reverted to Chinese control.

When a People's Republic was proclaimed in China at the end of the civil war, foreigners and Chinese industrialists, fleeing communism, left Shanghai, many re-establishing themselves in Hong Kong.

Because of its long history of foreign capitalist exploitation and 'bourgeois attitudes', adherents of the Cultural Revolution in the 1960s and '70s were particularly vociferous in Shanghai, which became the headquarters of the so-called Gang of Four, the ultra-leftist elements of this chaotic period.

## *What to See in Shanghai*

Walking along Zhongshan Lu under the shade of sycamore, cedar and camphor trees, the tourist can enjoy the faded grandeur of old Shanghai, for this was the **Bund**, where the great trading houses and banks had their headquarters. **Dongfeng Hotel** was the old Shanghai Club, whose Long Bar was, in its heyday, the longest in the world. The Municipal People's Government of Shanghai offices are in the columned building which was the Hongkong and Shanghai Bank headquarters, built in 1921; the green-roofed **Peace Hotel** was the handsome Cathay Hotel, where Noel Coward wrote his play *Private Lives* in 1928. The Palace Hotel, opposite, now part of the Peace Hotel, was Sassoon House (named after one of Shanghai's Jewish tycoons). The **Bank of China** is in one of the few buildings still run by its original occupants. The garden side of the Bund, once a simple towpath, is thronged with Shanghai residents, who stroll about in the hot summer evenings and in the mornings practise *taijiquan* and martial arts. In the old days, British residents held Sunday afternoon concerts and promenaded there. Though the regulations of the International Settlement forbade Chinese (other than servants and nannies) as well as dogs from the Bund gardens, the infamous sign 'No Dogs or Chinese Allowed' never really existed. The waterfront building with the clock tower is the old Customs House.

**Nanjing Lu**, the main shopping street of Shanghai, is lined with over 340 shops selling goods of all descriptions and from all parts of China. Nanjing Lu passes People's Park and the Municipal Library, the site of the former racecourse. English-speaking Shanghainese gather here, especially on Sunday mornings, to practise amongst themselves.

Book stores — antiquarian and modern — are a speciality of **Fuzhou Lu**, as well as stationery and calligraphy accoutrements, though in earlier times it was a red-light district.

Another important shopping street is **Huaihai Lu**, which was the main street of the French Concession, then called Avenue Joffre.

Renmin Lu and Zhonghua Lu form the perimeters of the old city wall (destroyed in 1912) which enclosed the Chinese City. Still within this area, which includes the famous **Yu Garden**, visitors jostle in the ever-crowded alleys of the bazaar, whose small shops, restaurants and teahouses provide local specialities of all description. The narrow streets nearby reveal an intimate and fascinating picture of daily life.

### Former Residences of Revolutionary Leaders
Several buildings reflect the city's revolutionary history. In a two-storeyed building at the corner of Huangpi Lu and Xinye Lu, the Communist Party of China was founded in 1921; it is proudly shown to visitors as the site of the First National Congress of the Communist Party of China. The former residence (1946) of the late premier Zhou Enlai is situated at 73 Sinan Lu, while at 7 Xiangshan Lu, the founder of modern China, Dr Sun Yatsen, and his wife Madame Soong Ching-ling lived between 1918 and 1924. Madame Soong, who lived much of her life in Shanghai, was made honorary chairman of the People's Republic of China upon her death in 1981. Her residence at 1843 Huaihai Lu, furnished as it was in her lifetime, is open to the public. China's great revolutionary writer Lu Xun (1881−1936) lived in a three-storeyed house at 9 Dalu New Village, Shanyin Lu, from 1933 until his death.

### Yu Garden
This Garden of Leisurely Repose on the northeast side of the old Chinese City was first established in 1559 by a mandarin named Pan. Laid out by a landscape artist, Zhang Nanyang, it has become one of the most renowed gardens in southern China. As the Pan family fortunes declined, the garden was neglected and overgrown until it was restored in 1760 by the local gentry. It became the headquarters of the Dagger Society in 1853, during the early part of the Taiping Rebellion, and was badly damaged. Part of the garden became the bazaar and local guildhalls, but over 20,000 square metres (24,000 square yards) remain of tall rockeries, halls, ponds and pavilions linked by zigzag corridors. The Spring Hall, used by the Dagger Society, houses exhibits of coins and weapons from that period. The five-ton porous **Exquisite Jade Rock** is one of the attractions: legend claims that when it was discovered some 900 years ago, it joined Emperor Huizong's collection of weird and grotesque rocks before finding a resting place in Yu Garden. Beside the garden is the famous five-sided **Huxinting (Heart-of-Lake Pavilion)** teahouse situated in the middle of a small lake and reached by a twisting wooden bridge. In 1842 the British forces made their headquarters in this teahouse and billeted their troops in the nearby Temple of the City God.

### Yufu (Jade Buddha) Monastery  Anyuan Lu
The yellow-walled monastery was established on this site in 1928. Its two jade buddhas (out of five brought back from Burma in 1882 by the

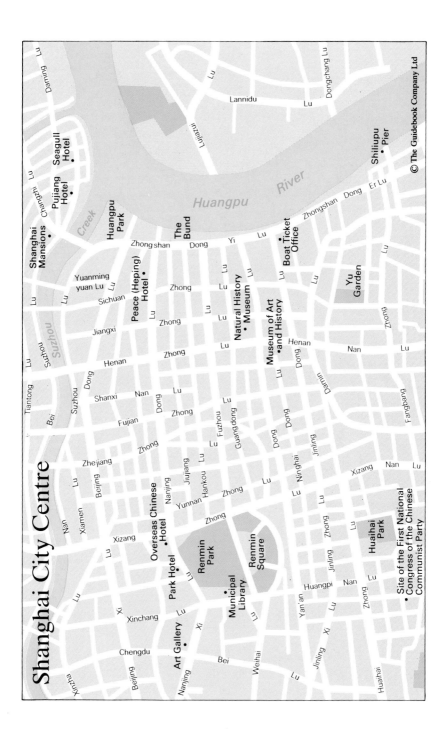

Shanghai City Centre

© The Guidebook Company Ltd

Huangpu River

Creek

Suzhou Creek

Daming Lu

Changzhi Lu

Seagull Hotel

Pujiang Hotel

Shanghai Mansions

Yuanming yuan Lu

Sichuan

Jiangxi

Henan

Suzhou Lu

Tiantong Lu

Bei

Zhejiang

Beijing

Lu

Xiamen

Nan

Lu

Xizang

Xinchang

Chengdu

Xinzha

Nanjing

Beijing

Art Gallery

Xi

Lu

Park Hotel

Overseas Chinese Hotel

Nanjing

Yunnan

Jiujiang

Hankou

Zhong

Renmin Park

Municipal Library

Renmin Square

Weihai

Bei

Yan'an

Huaihai

Jinling

Xi

Lu

Jinling

Nan

Lu

Zhong

Huangpi

Nan

Lu

Zhong

Huaihai Park

Site of the First National Congress of the Chinese Communist Party

Xizang

Nan

Lu

Ninghai

Jinling

Dong

Guangdong

Fuzhou

Lu

Zhong

Lu

Dawu

Dong

Henan

Dong

Museum of Art and History

Natural History Museum

Zhong

Lu

Zhong

Lu

Zhong

Shanxi

Nan

Dong

Fujian

Zhong

Peace (Heping) Hotel

Zhong shan

The Bund

Dong

Yi

Lu

Boat Ticket Office

Zhongshan Dong Er Lu

Shiliupu Pier

Yu Garden

Zhong

Nan

Lu

Fangbang

Huangpu Park

Lannidu

Lujiazui

Dongchang Lu

Lu

priest Hui Gen) were first kept in a suburb of Shanghai. Three halls
make up the monastery complex. In the Jade Buddha Hall is the
tranquil two-metre (6.5-foot) high seated statue of Sakyamuni, while
downstairs in the Reclining Buddha Hall is the white jade image of
Sakyamuni in repose. Precious statues of the Northern Wei and Tang
dynasties are on display in the monastery's exhibition hall, along with
hand-copied Tang-Dynasty Buddhist scriptures and paintings. Over 70
monks hold daily services. The monastery runs a vegetarian restaurant
whose menu boasts pickled duck, sliced eel, chicken and other 'meat'
dishes, all made of beancurd and vegetables. Crackling rice and
mushroom soup is recommended.

**Shanghai Museum of Art and History** Yan'an Lu
With a collection of over 100,000 objects, this museum is the richest in
China. Its superb bronzes, including wine vessels, containers and
ceremonial cooking utensils, date from the Shang and Zhou Dynasties
(*c.*16th—third century BC); pieces from this collection have been
exhibited extensively abroad. Painting and calligraphy from masters of
the Jin Dynasty on, including examples of Yangzhou's Eight Eccentrics
school, are on display. Pottery and porcelain exhibits date from the
Neolithic Age through to the contemporary period. The museum shop
sells reproductions of some of the paintings, porcelain and other relics.
Across the street is the **Shanghai Museum of Natural Sciences**.

## Longhua Pagoda and Temple

Situated in Shanghai's southwest area, the pagoda and temple were originally built between the tenth and the 13th centuries — historical records vary as to the exact dates. The present seven-storeyed pagoda is just over 40 metres (130 feet) high and dates from the early Song Dynasty, but was restored at the end of the Qing. The Longhua Temple nearby is a complex of five halls flanked by bell and drum towers; the sound of the evening bell of Longhua was known as one of the old traditions of Shanghai. A flower terrace, overlooked from a tea-room, is also one of the attractions of the temple, for in its peony gardens there is a 100-year old peony said to have been planted first in a Hangzhou temple during the reign of Emperor Xianfeng and later transplanted here. Engravings on a boundary stone indicate that the stone was placed at the southwest corner of this temple during the Five Dynasties period. West of the temple is **Longhua Park**, once part of the temple's peach orchard, and now replanted and expanded.

## Shanghai Botanical Gardens

South of the Longhua Pagoda, the gardens' greenhouses, bamboo groves and flower gardens cover some 67 hectares (165 acres) of land. Among the gardens' miniature *pengjing* trees is a pomegranate over 240 years old.

## Shanghai Zoo  Hongqiao Lu, near the airport

The zoo houses over 350 species of animals including giant pandas from Sichuan, golden-haired monkeys — which once frequented the Yangzi gorges — and rare Yangzi River alligators.

## Day Excursions from Shanghai

### Songjiang County

One of the attractions of the town of Songjiang, a county seat for over 2,500 years and situated 19 kilometres (12 miles) southwest of Shanghai, is the beautiful square brick and wood pagoda which is 900 years old. It is over 48 metres (157 feet) high with nine storeys and was once part of Xingshengjiao Temple, of which one hall remains. There is also a Tang-Dynasty stele, engraved with Buddhist scriptures, lions' heads, lotus petals and cloud patterns. It is said that the stele was erected to redeem the souls of criminals who were executed here. A lovely example of a classical Chinese garden, with bizarre rocks, ponds and miniature landscaping, can be seen on a visit to Zhuibaichi Park. This once-private garden probably dates from the late Ming Dynasty and became the villa of a painter, Gu Dashen, in the mid-17th century. In Songjiang the local speciality is the Four-grilled Perch, which is rather rare and has been known for centuries as 'the number one dish south of the Yangzi'. Emperor Yang of the Sui Dynasty praised the fish, saying it was 'as precious as gold and jade', while the Qing emperor Qianlong had four-grilled perch sent to him annually.

**Jiading County**
Twenty-five kilometres (15.5 miles) northwest of Shanghai is Jiading County, where a Confucian temple has existed since the 13th century. In the courtyard, steles set into plinths of stone turtles record the temple restorations and meritorious deeds of various officials. Three old cypress trees are all that are left of 60 planted in the Yuan Dynasty (1279—1368). Memorial tablets of Confucius' disciples and records of the achievements of local scholars line two corridors, which are part of the county museum. Five streams converge at the site of the **Huilong Tan (Pool of Convergent Dragons)**, and adorning the surrounding stone railings are 72 different lions (Confucius had 72 disciples). During the Taiping Rebellion, the soldiers of the Dagger Society were bound to the beautiful trees beside the pool and executed. Yingkui Hill in the centre of the pool dates from the Ming Dynasty, while the Literary God Tower, on the eastern bank, was restored recently after being bombed in the Sino-Japanese War. The **Garden of Autumn Clouds (Qiuxia Pu)**, near Huilong Pool, is another example of private garden architecture. This was laid out by a Minister of Defence, Gong Hong, in around 1520.

Another garden, **Guyi (Garden of Ancient Splendour)**, built by a high official of the Ming Dynasty, can be seen at the town of **Nanxiang**. Nanxiang dumplings are famous in the area, their skin being especially thin. Chen He set up his dumpling shop 100 years ago and his recipe was so successful that the dumplings took on the name of the town, rather than of his shop.

**Qingpu County**
A tourist resort centred on the **Dianshan Lake**, which feeds the Huangpu River, lies some 50 kilometres (31 miles) southwest of Shanghai. The lake covers some 6,300 hectares (15,570 acres) and is rich in mandarin fish, black carp, crab and freshwater shrimps.

On the shores of Daying Lake in Qingpu County is the **Garden of Meandering Stream (Qushui)**, which was built with funds donated by local townsfolk in 1745.

# Practical Information

## *Hotels in Chongqing*

扬子江假日酒店　重庆南岸庙区南坪乡
**Holiday Inn Yangtze** Nanping Xiang, Nanan
Chongqing's first international-style hotel (opening October 1988) is located on the southern bank of the river in an area designated for business development. Facilities include a swimming pool, health club, shops and a variety of restaurants.

重庆饭店　新华路41-43号
**Chungking Hotel (Chongqing Fandian)** 41−43 Xinhua Lu. Tel. 49301, tlx. 62193, cable 7315
Managed by a Hong Kong company, this is a well-run hotel, conveniently located in the city centre. Facilities include a beauty salon, a coffee shop serving Western food, and, in a second building, a business centre and small offices for rent to foreign businessmen.

人民宾馆　人民路175号
**Renmin Guesthouse** 175 Renmin Lu. Tel. 351421, tlx. 62127, fax. 352076
A monumental building with a tiered circular roof like the Temple of Heaven in Beijing, this is Chongqing's grand hotel. An extension formed by a new east wing, scheduled to open by late 1988, will double its room count.

渝州宾馆　袁家角友谊路
**Yuzhou Guesthouse** Youyi Lu, Yuanjiajiao. Tel. 811519, tlx. 62201
This hotel is to the northeast of the city and rather a long way from the centre of Chongqing.

重庆宾馆　中山一路
**Chongqing Guesthouse** Zhongshan Yi Lu. Tel. 53158, 46771, tlx. 62122
Not to be confused with Chungking Hotel. This hotel is used mainly by overseas Chinese.

## *Restaurants in Chongqing*

Sichuan cuisine is one of the four principal styles of Chinese cooking (the others are Cantonese, Peking and Huaiyang). The cuisine is characterized by hot piquant dishes heavily laced with red chillies, ginger and other condiments. Favourite local dishes include 'mother-in-law beancurd' (*mapo doufu*), double-cooked pork, diced chicken with hot peppers, *dandan* noodles, sour and hot soup, deep-fried beef strips and camphor-smoked duck.

老四川　八一路11号
**Lao Sichuan** 11 Bayi Lu. Tel. 41947
Specializes in beef dishes.

会仙楼　民族路184号
**Huixian Lou**  184 Minzu Lu. Tel. 51486

颐之时　解放碑
**Yizhishi Restaurant**  Jiefang Bei (People's Liberation Monument). Tel. 42680

## Useful Addresses in Chongqing

中国国际旅行社／中国旅行社　江北
**China International Travel Service/China Travel Service**  Jiangbei. Tel. 51556, 51449, tlx. 62126, cable 4015

重庆工艺服务部　解放碑
**Chongqing Arts and Crafts Service**  Jiefang Bei (People's Liberation Monument). Tel. 42797

重庆长江轮船公司
中国国际旅行社长江重庆支社
**Chongqing Changjiang Shipping Company**
**CITS Changjiang Chongqing Sub-branch**  4 Shaanxi Lu. Tel. 45942, tlx. 62200, cable 4239

重庆长江航客运站售票处　朝天门
**Chongqing Harbour Passenger Terminal**  (ticket office for Yangzi River passenger boats) Chaotianmen

重庆长途汽车站　牛角沱
**Chongqing Long Distance Bus Station**  Niujiaotuo. Tel. 52149

重庆火车站　菜元坝
**Chongqing Railway Station**  Caiyuanba. Ticket desk tel. 53927, enquiries tel. 52607

## Hotel in Wanxian

太白宾馆　白岩路30号
**Taibai Guesthouse**  30 Baiyan Lu. Tel. 3976
An air-conditioned, 36-room hotel with a pleasant view and good Sichuan cuisine.

## Shopping in Wanxian

工艺美术商店　三马路1号
**Arts and Crafts Store**  1 San Malu

万县文物商店　电报路111号
**Wanxian Antiques Shop** 111 Dianbao Lu. Tel. 3913

## *Restaurant in Fengjie*

金龙酒家　月牙街３号
**Golden Dragon Restaurant** (Jinlong Jiujia) 3 Yueya Jie
Opened in the year of the dragon (1988), this restaurant serves traditional
Sichuan food. The Golden Dragon also offers some guestrooms with attached
baths.

## *Hotel in Wushan*

Wushan is not yet geared to take large groups of foreign tourists, and those
tours which have the Daning River excursion on their itinerary normally just
stop here for the day.

巫峡宾馆　集仙街72号
**Wuxia Guesthouse** 72 Jixian Jie. Tel. 226
A five-storey hotel, recently completed, offers air-conditioned twin rooms
(with attached bathrooms) and dormitory accommodation. The Foreign Affairs
Office of Wushan County, which doubles as the Tourism Bureau, is located at
this modest guesthouse.

## *Hotels in Yichang*

三峡宾馆　沿江路
**Three Gorges Hotel** (Sanxia Binguan) Yanjiang Lu. Tel. 23438, 24911, tlx.
40253
Opened in 1987, this is at present Yichang's most modern and well-appointed
hotel.

桃花岭饭店　云集路29号
**Taohualing Hotel** 29 Yunji Lu. Tel. 22515, 23812
A garden-style hotel in the downtown area. In the grounds are three old
houses of the Treaty Port days.

南湖饭店　福绥路62号
**Nanhu Hotel** 62 Fusui Lu. Tel. 24033, 24067

彝岭饭店　云集路67号
**Yiling Hotel** 67 Yunji Lu. Tel. 23611

葛洲坝饭店　东山大道82号
**Gezhouba Hotel** 82 Dongshan Dadao. Tel. 22011, 22050

## *Restaurants in Yichang*

**松鹤村**　解放路84号
**Pine and Crane Village (Songhecun)** 84 Jiefang Lu. Tel. 23729

**陶珠饭店**　解放路13号
**Taozhu Restaurant** 13 Jiefang Lu. Tel. 21288

**三峡饭店**　二马路46号
**Three Gorges Restaurant** 46 Er Malu. Tel. 22483

## *Useful Addresses in Yichang*

**中国银行(宜昌支行)**　东山大道147号
**Bank of China Yichang Sub-branch** 147 Dongshan Dadao. Tel. 22635

**中国国际旅行社三峡支社**　三峡宾馆
**China International Travel Service (Three Gorges Sub-Branch)** Three Gorges Hotel. Tel. 24196, tlx. 40253, cable 1650

**中国国际旅行社宜昌分社**　桃花岭饭店
**China International Travel Service (Yichang Branch)** Taohualing Hotel compound. Tel. 22515 ext. 597

**中国民航售票处**　夷陵大道167号
**Civil Aviation Administration of China (CAAC) Ticket Office** 167 Yiling Dadao. Tel. 22648

**长江航客运宜昌站售票处**　沿江大道273号
**Yangzi Passenger Terminal Ticket Office** 273 Yanjiang Dadao. Tel. 21245

**宜昌火车站售票处**　山庄路1-8号
**Yichang Railway Station Ticket Office** 1−8 Shanzhuang Lu. Tel. 21504

## *Hotels in Wuhan*

**长江大酒店**　解放大道
**Yangtze Hotel** Jiefang Dadao, Hankou. Tel. 562828, tlx. 40204, fax. 353759, cable 2700
The best hotel in Wuhan, recently opened and run by Hong Kong managers. Excellent Cantonese and local Hubei cuisine restaurant on the eighth floor.

**晴川饭店**　洗马长街88号
**Qingchuan Hotel** 88 Ximachang Jie. Tel. 444361, 441141, tlx. 40134, cable 8550
CITS put their groups here. Location pleasant but out of the way. Guests can walk out of the hotel and straight on to the cruise boat *Yangtzekiang*, which is usually moored right in front of the hotel

胜利饭店　汉口四唯路
**Victory Hotel (Shengli Fandian)** 11 Siwei Lu, Hankou. Tel. 512780
This hotel is one of several older establishments in the city. The public areas
are dark and gloomy but renovation is about to be carried out.

江汉饭店　汉口胜利路245号
**Jianghan Hotel** 245 Shengli Jie, Hankou. Tel. 21253, tlx. 40150
Old-fashioned façade and internal furnishings which recall the foreign presence
in Hankou in the late 19th century. A newly renovated wing provides
accommodation with modern bathrooms.

璇宫饭店　汉口江汉一路45号
**Xuangong Hotel** 45 Jianghan Yi Lu, Hankou. Tel. 21023

汉口饭店　汉口解放大道
**Hankou Hotel** Jiefang Dadao, Hankou. Tel. 56941, tlx. 40203

## *Restaurants in Wuhan*

老通城酒家　汉口大智路１号
**Laotongcheng** 1 Dazhi Lu, Hankou. Tel. 24559

老大兴园酒家　利济北路219号
**Laodaxingyuan Jiujia** 219 Liji Bei Lu

## *Useful Addresses in Wuhan*

中国国际旅行社武汉分社　江汉一路48号
**China International Travel Service (CITS) Wuhan Branch** 48 Jianghan Yi Lu,
Hankou. Tel. 25649, 23505, 25018, tlx. 40211, cable 1954

中国国际旅行社长江分社　沿江大道89号
**China International Travel Service (CITS) Changjiang Branch** 89 Yanjiang
Dadao. Tel. 511049, tlx. 40132, cable 4830

中国武汉长江轮船公司
中国国际旅行社长江武汉支社
长江武汉中国旅行社　汉口沿江大道67号
**China Wuhan Changjiang Shipping Company**
**China International Travel Service, Changjiang Wuhan Sub-branch**
**Changjiang Wuhan China International Service** 67 Yanjiang Dadao, Hankou.
Tel. 354704, tlx. 40258, cable. 4110

湖北外文书店　中南路
**Hubei Foreign Language Bookstore** Zhongnan Lu. Tel. 812791, 812746,
812818

长江航客运站　汉口沿江大道80号
**Yangzi Passenger Terminal** 80 Yanjiang Dadao, Hankou. *Ticket Office* tel.
53207 *Information* tel. 353875

中国民航　武汉利济北路217号
**Civil Aviation Administration of China (CAAC)** 217 Liji Bei Lu, Hankou.
*Ticket Office* tel. 56780

汉口飞机场　汉口
**Hankou Airport** Hankou. Tel. 55174

汉口长途汽车站　汉口解放大道403号
**Hankou Long Distance Bus Station** 403 Jiefang Dadao, Hankou. Tel. 52444

南湖机场　武昌
**Nanhu Airport** Wuchang. Tel. 73650

武昌火车站　武昌
**Wuchang Railway Station** Wuchang. Tel. 71161

## Hotel in Jiujiang

南湖宾馆　南司路77号
**Nanhu Guesthouse** 77 Nansi Lu. Tel. 2272
This pleasant large guesthouse with garden on the shores of Gantang Lake is about 15 minutes' walk from the town centre.

## Restaurants in Jiujiang

观湖楼　甘棠湖
**Guanhu Lou** Gantang Lake
This picturesquely sited restaurant overlooks Gantang Lake and the Yanshui Pavilion. The food is very good. Try deep-fried Mandarin fish (*Songshu yu*), tiny prawns, crispy rice, and vegetables in season.

南湖宾馆　南司路77号
**Nanhu Guesthouse Restaurant** 77 Nansi Lu. Tel. 2272

## Useful Address in Jiujiang

中国国际旅行社　南司路77号
**China International Travel Service** 77 Nansi Lu. Tel. 2526

## Hotel in Wuhu

铁山宾馆　更新路
**Tieshan Guesthouse (Iron Hill Guesthouse)** Gengxin Lu. Tel. 3920
This is the main hotel for foreigners. The hotel restaurant serves an excellent crab soup and fresh crabs in the autumn.

# Hotels in Nanjing

金陵饭店　新街口汉中路2号
**Jinling Hotel** 2 Hanzhong Lu, Xinjiekou. Tel. 44141, 41221, tlx. 34110, fax.
(025)43396
This 37-storey hotel provides international-standard accommodation and
services. It has Western and Chinese restaurants and a revolving Sky Palace
bar with a panoramic view of the city.

丁山宾馆　察哈尔路90号
**Dingshan Guesthouse** 90 Chaha'er Lu. Tel. 85931, tlx. 34103
A complex of buildings set in spacious grounds, the Dingshan offers a range of
accommodation from recently renovated first-class guestrooms to cheaper
lodgings in two blocks of prefabricated buildings.

南京饭店　中山北路25
**Nanjing Hotel** 259 Zhongshan Bei Lu. Tel. 34121, tlx. 34102
Standard accommodation in garden-style hotel built in the 1950s.

双门楼宾馆　虎踞北路185号
**Shuangmenlou Guesthouse** 185 Huju Bei Lu. Tel. 85961, tlx. 34118
Another sprawling complex which contains the former British Consulate
building (now quite shabby). The main building of this hotel has been
modernized.

玄武饭店　中央路193号
**Xuanwu Hotel** 193 Zhongyang Lu. Tel. 38121, 39191, tlx. 34026, 34042
A new hotel with good location on the west side of Xuanwu Lake Park.

# Restaurants in Nanjing

Food in Nanjing's major hotels is usually of a high standard. Regional
specialities include Nanjing pressed duck, mandarin fish stuffed with shrimp,
and spare ribs in a rich soyabean sauce. Cooking styles from other parts of
China may also be sampled in Nanjing. The restaurants in the Fuzi Miao area,
off Jiankang Lu south of the city centre, are worth trying for their Jiangsu fare.
These restaurants include the Qifangge and Yongheyuan (see below).

大三元　中山路38号
**Dasanyuan** 38 Zhongshan Lu. Tel. 49027
Well-established Cantonese restaurant.

南京烤鸭馆　中山北路151号
**Nanjing Roast Duck Restaurant** 151 Zhongshan Bei Lu. Tel. 33725
Serves the ever-popular Beijing duck and other northern dishes.

老广东菜馆　中山路45号
**Old Cantonese Restaurant** (Lao Guangdong) 45 Zhongshan Lu. Tel. 42482.

**奇芳阁** 贡院街150号
**Qifangge** 150 Gongyuan Jie. Tel. 23159

**四川饭店** 太平南路171号
**Sichuan Restaurant** 171 Taiping Nan Lu. Tel. 46651
A restaurant serving the typically hot and spicy food of Sichuan. Recently
enlarged and refurbished.

**永和园** 贡院街122号
**Yongheyuan** 122 Gongyuan Jie. Tel. 23863

## Shopping in Nanjing

Zhongshan Lu and Xinjiekou are the main shopping boulevards of the city,
and the People's Market (Renmin Shangchang) at 79 Zhongshan Nan Lu is the
most centrally located department store. A vast emporium (Nanjing
Shangchang) was recently opened in the north of the city; from this four-
storeyed store you can get an interesting glimpse into the consumer side of
contemporary Chinese life. From thermos flasks to refrigerators, its wares
draw crowds of Nanjing's citizens as well as visitors from other provinces and
the increasingly affluent townships in the Jiangsu countryside. Nanjing is also
the source of Yunjin brocade — one of three main types made in China.
Woven of fine gold and silver silk thread, it is decorative and ornate.

**聚宝斋** 汉中路9号
**Collected Treasures Antique Store (Jubaozhai)** 9 Hanzhong Lu. Tel. 44550

**外文书店** 中山东路137号
**Foreign Languages Bookstore** 137 Zhongshan Dong Lu. Tel. 43718

**友谊商店** 中央路
**Friendship Store** Zhongyang Lu. Tel. 32802

**江苏文物商店** 中山门
**Jiangsu Antique Store** Zhongshanmen. Tel. 41895

**金陵饭店小卖部** 新街口汉中路2号
**Jinling Hotel (lobby shop and shopping arcade)** 2 Hanzhong Lu, Xinjiekou.
Tel. 44141
The hotel lobby shop sells imported spirits, chocolates, film, postcards. A
separate shopping arcade houses a number of stores for handicrafts, souvenirs,
English-language books, antiques etc.

## Useful Addresses in Nanjing

**中国银行** 中山东路3号
**Bank of China** 3 Zhongshan Dong Lu. Tel. 48065, *Foreign department* 49280

中国国际旅行社　中山北路202-1号
**China International Travel Service (CITS)** 202−1 Zhongshan Bei Lu. Tel. 48889, 47792

中国国际旅行社金陵饭店支社　新街口汉中路2号
**CITS Sub-branch** Jinling Hotel, 2 Hanzhong Lu, Xinjiekou. Tel. 41121

中国民航售票处　瑞金路2号
**Civil Aviation Administration of China (CAAC) (Booking office)** 52 Ruijin Lu. Tel. (Passenger) 43378

南京商场　昭山路2号
**Nanjing Emporium (Nanjing Shangchang)** 2 Zhaoshan Lu. Tel. 52407

南京火车站　昭山路
**Nanjing Railway Station** Zhaoshan Lu. Tel. 51294

## Hotels in Zhenjiang

金山饭店　金山路1号
**Jinshan Hotel** 1 Jinshan Xi Lu. Tel. 24961, 24962, cable 6333

一泉饭店　一泉路
**First Spring Guesthouse** (Yiquan Binguan) Yiquan Lu. Tel. 23152

## Restaurants in Zhenjiang

Restaurants in Zhenjiang are very basic establishments unequipped to cater to foreign guests, so visitors are confined to the dining room at the Jinshan Hotel. Zhenjiang specialities include steamed crab roe dumplings in soup, casseroled crabmeat with minced pork balls, Zhenjiang shad (in season in the spring) and shredded beancurd in chicken soup.

## Shopping in Zhenjiang

文物商店　解放路191号
**Antique Store** 191 Jiefang Lu. Tel. 22335

友谊商店　解放路105号
**Friendship Store** 105 Jiefang Lu. Tel. 21478

## Useful Addresses in Zhenjiang

中国银行镇江分行　东门广场
**Bank of China Zhenjiang Branch** Dongmen Guangchang. Tel. 21202

中国国际旅行社　健康路25号
**China International Travel Service**　25 Jiankang Lu. Tel. 23281

电讯营业处　新马路3号
**Posts and Telegraph Office**　3 Xin Malu. Tel. 21237

镇江外事办公室　小码头街21号
**Zhenjiang Foreign Affairs Office**　21 Xiao Matou Jie. Tel. 22143

## Hotels in Yangzhou

扬州宾馆　丰乐上街5号
**Yangzhou Guesthouse**　5 Fengle Shang Jie. Tel. 42611 ext. 453, 454

西园饭店　丰乐上街1号
**Xiyuan Hotel**　1 Fengle Shang Jie. Tel. 42611 ext. 590, 591

## Restaurants in Yangzhou

Yangzhou delicacies, appreciated for 1,000 years, were classified in the Qing Dynasty as one of the four main regional cuisines of China, known as the Huaiyang (the others being Cantonese, Sichuanese and Beijing). Much store is placed on presentation, fragrance and freshness. Full use is made of the products from this 'Land of Fish and Rice' — prawns, crab, shad, mullet, duck, game, lotus seeds and roots.

Yangzhou specialities include Yangzhou fried rice, palace lantern shrimps, drunken crab, wine-lees mandarin fish, steamed crab 'lions' heads', three-fowl stew, hibiscus duck slices, scholar's beancurd and double-yolk duck eggs.

Old folks in Yangzhou customarily eat breakfast in restaurants; why not sample this delightful experience at the famous old **Fuchun Chashe** (35 Desheng Qiao, off Guoqing Lu) and walk through the kitchens piled with mountains of steamers containing a wide variety of dumplings?

The **Yangzhou Guesthouse** has several dining rooms where a banquet of Huaiyang specialities can be arranged.

## Shopping in Yangzhou

友谊商店　国庆北路454号
**Friendship Store**　454 Guoqing Bei Lu. Tel. 21631

扬州文物商店　盐阜路1号
**Yangzhou Antique and Curio Store**　1 Yanfu Lu. Tel. 24987

扬州工艺厂　汶河路141号
**Yangzhou Arts and Crafts Factory**　141 Wenhe Lu. Tel. 23718

扬州玉器厂　广储门外街6号
**Yangzhou Jade Factory**　6 Guangchumenwai Jie. Tel. 21965

扬州漆器厂　沿河街50号
**Yangzhou Lacquerware Factory**　50 Yanhe Jie. Tel. 21127

## Useful Addresses in Yangzhou

中国银行扬州分社　盐阜路 8 号
**Bank of China Yangzhou Branch** 8 Yanfu Lu. Tel. 43885, 42291

中国国际旅行社　丰乐上街1号
**China International Travel Service** 1 Fengle Shang Jie. Tel. 42611 ext. 392, tlx. 34075

## Hotels in Shanghai

The notorious shortage of accommodation encountered by visitors to the city in recent years will be dramatically reversed with the opening of many new hotels, some of them joint ventures with foreign companies. The hotels built in the 1920s and 1930s, however, remain delightfully old-fashioned with wooden panelling, chandeliers and ornate pillars; some are converted apartment buildings. Below is a selection of the choice available, or soon to be available.

*Modern luxury-standard hotels*

华亭宾馆　漕西北路1200号
**Huating Sheraton** 1200 Caoxi Bei Lu. Tel. 386000, tlx. 33589
The first hotel in Shanghai to be managed by an international chain, the Sheraton has top-class facilities including indoor swimming pool, conference facilities, gymnasium, tennis courts, and a bowling alley.

上海静安希尔顿酒店　华山路250号
**Shanghai Jing'an Hilton** 250 Huashan Lu. Tel. 550000, tlx. 33612, fax. 553848, cable HILTELS SHANGHAI
Opened in 1987, this hotel offers all the facilities associated with hotels of this class — swimming pool, executive business centre, health club and several permutations of restaurants and bars. There are 777 guestrooms.

上海日航龙柏饭店　虹桥路2451号
**Nikko Longbai** 2451 Hongqiao Lu. Tel. 593636, tlx. 30138
Located in the western suburbs, this is managed by Nikko Hotels International (not to be confused with the Cypress Hotel or Longbai Fandian at 2419 Hongqiao Lu).

上海天鹅信谊宾馆　江湾路111号
**Swan Cindic Hotel** 111 Jiangwan Lu. Tel. 255255, tlx. 30023
Overlooks Hongkou Park.

天马大酒店　吴中路471号
**Tianma Hotel** 471 Wuzhong Lu. Tel. 328100, tlx. 30901, cable 89002
Middle-range hotel, located in the western suburbs and opened in 1988.

Other hotels in the process of construction or planning, with projected opening dates stretching into the early 1990s, include the Shanghai International

Airport Hotel, City Hotel, Ocean Hotel, Yangtze River Hotel, Garden Hotel, Jinjiang Tower (see Jinjiang Hotel below), Hyatt Shanghai, Pacific Shanghai, and the Portman.

*Old-style hotels*

锦江饭店　茂名南路59号
**Jinjiang Hotel** 59 Maoming Nan Lu. Tel. 582582, tlx. 33380
This hotel complex includes the grand north block, with its curving steps leading up to the columned entrance, which dates from 1931. It was then in the centre of the French quarter. Buildings added later have expanded the hotel so that it now offers some 800 rooms and several shops. A new extension, Jinjiang Tower, complete with swimming pool and revolving restaurant, will open in 1989.

和平饭店　南京东路20号
**Peace Hotel** 20 Nanjing Dong Lu. Tel. 211244
This interesting hotel was built in 1928 and was then known as the Cathay. Its distinctive green roof is a landmark of the Bund. The former Palace Hotel across the road, built in 1906, now forms part of the Peace Hotel.

上海大厦　北苏州路20号
**Shanghai Mansions** 20 Bei Suzhou Lu. Tel. 244186, tlx. 33007
This was formerly the apartment-hotel complex known as Broadway Mansions, built in 1934. The American military advisory group to the Guomindang government was housed here, as was the Foreign Correspondents' Club.

静安宾馆　华山路370号
**Jing'an Guesthouse** 370 Huashan Lu. Tel. 563050
Previously the Haig Apartments, a smart private hotel for foreigners, the comfortable Jing'an is now a highly popular medium-price guesthouse with expanded accommodation in the new West Wing.

国际饭店　南京西路170号
**Park Hotel** 170 Nanjing Xi Lu. Tel. 225225
Built in 1934, when it overlooked the Racecourse, now People's Park, this hotel is also known as the Guoji (International). The view of the city from the upper-floor rooms is spectacular.

*Guesthouses*

There are a number of expensive guesthouses in Shanghai, catering to official, diplomatic and business delegations as well as special tour groups. They are normally complexes of old private houses set in large handsome gardens.

西郊宾馆　虹桥路1921号
**Western Suburbs Guesthouse (Xijiao Binguan)** 1921 Hongqiao Lu. Tel. 379643, tlx. 33004
Seven buildings in beautifully kept grounds.

虹桥迎宾馆　虹桥路1591号
**Hongqiao Guesthouse** 1591 Hongqiao Lu. Tel. 372170

**瑞金宾馆**　瑞金路118号
**Ruijin Guesthouse**　118 Ruijin Lu. Tel. 372653, tlx. 33603

**东湖宾馆**　新东路167号
**Donghu Guesthouse**　167 Xinle Lu. Tel. 370050

*Standard/budget hotels*

**新苑宾馆**　虹桥路1900号
**New Garden Hotel**　1900 Hongqiao Lu. Tel. 329000

**华桥饭店**　南京西路104号
**Overseas Chinese Hotel**　104 Nanjing Xi Lu. Tel. 226226

**上海宾馆**　乌鲁木齐北路505号
**Shanghai Hotel**　505 Wulumuqi Bei Lu. Tel. 312312, tlx. 33295

**海鸥饭店**　黄浦路60号
**Seagull Hotel (Hai'ou Fandian)**　60 Huangpu Lu. Tel. 251043, tlx. 33603

**浦江饭店**　黄浦路17号
**Pujiang Hotel**　17 Huangpu Lu. Tel. 246388

## Restaurants in Shanghai

As one might expect from such a city, almost every style of Chinese regional cuisine is available as well as a variety of European food. Shanghai freshwater crabs — in season between October and December — are so much in demand that they are flown to Chinese and Japanese gourmets overseas. In the old city bazaar (near the Yu Garden), all kinds of local snacks may be tried: sesame cakes, egg rolls, glutinous rice in lotus leaves, noodles, deep-fried dough sticks (*youtiao*), steamed bread and dumplings.

Apart from the restaurants in the major hotels — sometimes of varying standards — some of the popular regional Chinese restaurants are listed below.

*Shanghainese/Huaiyang*

**老饭店**　福佑路242号
**Lao Fandian**　242 Fuyou Lu. Tel. 282782
Near the Yu Garden in the old Chinese City, the Old Restaurant, as Lao Fandian translates, serves local food.

**扬州饭店**　南京东路308号
**Yangzhou Fandian**　308 Nanjing Dong Lu. Tel. 222779
This restaurant specializes in the local cuisine, offering Shanghainese dishes as well as those associated with Huaiyang, which is the cuisine of the surrounding province of Jiangsu. The Yangzhou is highly popular and reservations should be made in advance.

**甬江状元楼**　西藏中路162号
**Yongjiang Zhuangyuan Lou**　162 Xizang Zhong Lu. Tel. 225280
Seafood cooked in Ningbo style is the speciality of this restaurant.

*Sichuanese*

**梅龙镇酒家**　南京西路1081号
**Meilongzhen Jiujia** 22 Nanjing Xi Lu, 1081 Long (Lane). Tel. 532561
The most well-known Sichuanese restaurant in Shanghai.

**绿杨村**　南京东路763号
**Luyangcun** 763 Nanjing Dong Lu. Tel. 737221
Both Sichuanese and Shanghainese cuisine is available here.

Both the **Huating Sheraton** and the **Jinjiang Hotel** have restaurants offering Chinese dishes of a variety of cooking styles, including Sichuanese.

*Beijing and Shandong*

**国际饭店**　南京西路170号
**Park Hotel** 170 Nanjing Xi Lu. Tel. 225225
The Beijing-duck restaurant in this hotel is known as the Fengze.

*Cantonese*

**美心**　陕西南路
**Meixin Jiujia** 314 Shaanxi Nan Lu. Tel. 373919

**新雅**　南京东路719号
**Xinya** 719 Nanjing Dong Lu. Tel. 224393

**友谊酒家**　上海展览馆
**Friendship Restaurant (Youyi Jiujia)** Shanghai Exhibition Centre, 1000 Yan'an Zhong Lu. Tel. 534078

*Others*

The new top-class hotels all offer Western-style restaurants and coffee shops. For curiosity value, the **Red House (Hong Fangzi)**, 37 Shaanxi Nan Lu, tel. 565748, is worth a visit. It has been going since before the revolution, and was originally known as Chez Louis. The recent renovation has unfortunately reduced its period charm.

**香格里拉**　延安东路联谊大厦
**Shangri-la** Second Floor, Union Building, 100 Yan'an Dong Lu. Tel. 265230, 265480
A European restaurant in a highrise office block.

**悦宾沙嗲屋**　华山路249号
**VIP Satay House (Yuebin Shadie Wu)** 849 Huashan Lu. Tel. 312211
Indonesian restaurant run by an overseas Chinese.

**绿波廊餐厅**　豫园
**Lubolang Restaurant** Yu Garden Bazaar. Tel. 280602
Noodles, *jiaozi* (steamed dumplings) and pastries.

**天天快餐公司**　西藏中路68-74号
**T.T. Fastfood Service** 68-74 Xizang Zhong Lu. Tel. 265853
Hamburgers, hot dogs, lunch-box Chinese meals.

## Shopping in Shanghai

The Shanghai area is famous for many arts and crafts — paper-cutting, jade carving, Jiading straw weaving, ivory carving, lacquerware, and needlepoint (introduced at the turn of this century by Western missionaries). The tradition of Gu silk embroidery is over 300 years old. It began with a local official, Gu Mingshi, who was fond of giving silk embroideries, made by his concubines, as presents.

Huge department stores supply all kinds of Chinese-produced goods and are always packed with shoppers.

*Antiques, arts and crafts*

创新古玩店　淮海路1297号
**Chuangxin Old Wares Shop**　1297 Huaihai Lu

国华瓷器商店　南京东路550号
**Guohua Porcelain Shop**　550 Nanjing Dong Lu. Tel. 224526

南市刺绣商店　豫园新路21号
**Old Town Embroidery**　Shop 21 Yuyuan Xin Lu. Tel. 281611

上海文物商店　广东路218号
**Shanghai Antique and Curio Store**　218 Guangdong Lu. Tel. 212864

上海工艺美术品服务部　南京西路190号
**Shanghai Arts and Crafts Service Centre**　190 Nanjing Xi Lu. Tel. 537238

上海长江刻字厂　淮海中路722号
**Shanghai Changjiang Seal Carving Factory**　722 Huaihai Zhong Lu. Tel. 211854

*Book stores*

古籍书店　福州路424号
**China Classics Book Store**　424 Fuzhou Lu. Tel. 223453

外文书店　福州路380号
**Foreign Languages Book Store**　380 Fuzhou Lu. Tel. 224109

上海书店　福州路401-411号
**Shanghai Book Store**　401−11 Fuzhou Lu. Tel. 282894

新华书店　南京东路345号
**Xinhua Book Store**　345 Nanjing Dong Lu. Tel. 212599

*Department stores*

友谊商店　北京东路33号
**Friendship Store**　33 Beijing Dong Lu. Tel. 234600

上海第一百货公司　南京东路830号
**Shanghai No. 1 Department Store**　830 Nanjing Dong Lu. Tel. 223344

华联商厦　南京东路635号
**Hualian Department Store (previously the Shanghai No. 10 Department Store)** 635 Nanjing Dong Lu. Tel. 224466

*Painting and calligraphy*
文房四宝　茂名南路59号锦江饭店
**Four Treasures of the Study (Wenfang Sibao)** Jinjiang Hotel, 59 Maoming Nan Lu

*Others*
吉佳超级市场　茂名南路59号锦江饭店
**Jessica** Jinjiang Hotel, 59 Maoming Nan Lu
Imported toiletries, sweets, wines and spirits.

上海戏剧服装用品厂门市部　南京东路259号
**Theatre Costume Shop** 259 Nanjing Xi Lu

## Useful Addresses in Shanghai

中国东方航空公司　虹桥国际机场
**China Eastern Airlines** Hongqiao International Airport. Tel. 518550

中国国际旅行社　中山东一路33号
**China International Travel Service (CITS)** 33 Zhongshan Dong Yi Lu. Tel. 217200, tlx. 33277

中国旅行社　南京西路104号
**China Travel Service (CTS)** 104 Nanjing Xi Lu. Tel. 226226

中国青年旅行社　陕西南路5号
**China Youth Travel Service (CYTS)** 5 Shaanxi Nan Lu. Tel. 565613

虹桥飞机场
**Hongqiao Airport** Flight enquiries. Tel. 537664

浦江游览服务站　北京东路码头
**Huangpu River Tourism Service** Beijing Dong Lu Wharf. Tel. 211098

公安局外事科　汉口路210号
**Public Security Bureau Foreigners Section** 210 Hankou Lu. Tel. 211997

上海友谊汽车服务公司　长乐路400号
**Shanghai Friendship Taxi Company** 400 Changle Lu. Tel. 584584, 536363

上海站售票处　天目西路
**Shanghai Railway Ticket Office** Tianmu Xi Lu. Tel. 559090

上海出租汽车　北京东路816号
**Shanghai Taxi Service** 816 Beijing Dong Lu. Tel. 222999 (cars), 215555 (coaches), 580000 (mini-buses)

# Recommended Reading

The most interesting and graphic accounts of journeys up and down the Yangzi River are to be found in books by 19th- and early 20th-century European travellers, merchants and missionaries. While many of these titles are currently out of print, they can be found in good reference libraries.

Archibald Little spent most of his working life in China as a trader and pioneered steamship navigation on the upper reaches of the river. He wrote *Through the Yangtze Gorges* (1887) and *Gleanings from Fifty Years in China* (1908) — two vivid accounts of his experiences. His wife, Mrs Archibald Little, was a leading light in the Anti-Footbinding Movement in China, and also wrote several accounts of her life along the Yangzi: *Intimate China* and *In the Land of the Blue Gown* (1908).

*The Journey of August R. Margary* (1876) reveals the hardships of travel on the river in the late 19th century. Margary, a young British consular officer, made a remarkable journey alone, by river from Shanghai to Sichuan Province, and then by road through Yunnan Province to the Burmese border. On his return, he was murdered by tribesmen. George E. Morrison, the famous correspondent of *The Times* at the turn of the century, was an intrepid traveller. His entertaining book, *An Australian in China*, recalling his overland journey on a route similar to that of Margary's, is reprinted by Oxford University Press (1985).

Other accounts include *A Yankee on the Yangtze* (1904) by William Edgar Geil, *My Boating and Shooting Excursions to the Gorges of the Upper Yangtze* (1889) by W.S. Percival, and *Five Months on the Yangtze* by T.W. Blakeston (1832–91).

Missionary accounts include *The Yangtze and the Yak* (Edwards Brothers, Inc., Michigan, 1952) by Marion H. Duncan, and *In the Valley of the Yangtze* (London Missionary Society, 1899) by Mrs Arnold Foster.

*Sail and Sweep in China* (British Science Museum, 1966) by G.R.G. Worcester, a former river inspector of the Chinese Maritime Customs, is a detailed account of the types of boats which frequented the rivers of China.

Two publications, *In Search of Old Shanghai* by Pan Ling (Joint Publishing Company, Hong Kong, 1982) and *In Search of Old Nanjing* by Barry Till (Joint Publishing Company, Hong Kong, 1982) are detailed histories of these cities and their sights.

Arthur Waley's *The Poetry and Career of Li Po* (George Allen & Unwin, 1969) — about one of China's best loved Tang-Dynasty poets — describes the life of officials and their travels from post to post during the eighth century. Wu Ching-tzu's *The Scholars*, a Qing-

Dynasty novel of official manners, translated by Yang Hsien-yi and Gladys Yang (Foreign Languages Press, Beijing, 1973), contains accounts of river journeys and drinking-and-poetry boating parties enjoyed by the literati throughout China's history.

*Romance of the Three Kingdoms* (Charles E. Tuttle Co., Inc., 1973) — the 14th-century novel about three warring states by Luo Guanzhong — is a classic of Chinese literature. In *Excerpts from Three Classical Chinese Novels*, published by Panda Books (Beijing, 1981), there is a translation of *The Battle of the Red Cliff* (excerpted from *Romance of the Three Kingdoms*), that vividly decribes this event at a site just above Wuhan.

# Table of Distances between Main Yangzi River Ports

Distances in kilometres (miles)

| Chongqing | Chongqing | | | | | | | | | |
|---|---|---|---|---|---|---|---|---|---|---|
| Wanxian | 327 (203) | Wanxian | | | | | | | | |
| Fengjie | 446 (277) | 119 (74) | Fengjie | | | | | | | |
| Yichang | 648 (403) | 321 (200) | 202 (126) | Yichang | | | | | | |
| Shashi | 815 (506) | 488 (303) | 369 (229) | 167 (104) | Shashi | | | | | |
| Wuhan | 1354 (841) | 1027 (638) | 908 (564) | 706 (439) | 539 (335) | Wuhan | | | | |
| Jiujiang | 1623 (1008) | 1296 (805) | 1177 (731) | 975 (606) | 808 (502) | 269 (167) | Jiujiang | | | |
| Wuhu | 1991 (1237) | 1664 (1034) | 1545 (960) | 1343 (835) | 1176 (731) | 637 (396) | 368 (229) | Wuhu | | |
| Nanjing | 2087 (1297) | 1760 (1094) | 1641 (1020) | 1439 (894) | 1272 (790) | 733 (455) | 464 (288) | 96 (60) | Nanjing | |
| Zhenjiang | 2174 (1351) | 1847 (1148) | 1728 (1074) | 1526 (948) | 1359 (844) | 820 (510) | 551 (342) | 183 (114) | 87 (54) | Zhenjiang |
| Shanghai | 2479 (1540) | 2152 (1337) | 2033 (1263) | 1831 (1138) | 1664 (1034) | 1125 (699) | 856 (532) | 488 (303) | 392 (244) | 305 (190) | Shanghai |

# Chronology of Periods in Chinese History

| | |
|---|---|
| Palaeolithic | *c.*600,000−7000 BC |
| Neolithic | *c.*7000−1600 BC |
| Shang | *c.*1600−1027 BC |
| Western Zhou | 1027−771 BC |
| Eastern Zhou | 770−256 BC |
|    Spring and Autumn Annals | 770−476 BC |
|    Warring States | 475−221 BC |
| Qin | 221−207 BC |
| Western (Former) Han | 206 BC−AD 8 |
| Xin | 9−24 |
| Eastern (Later) Han | 25−220 |
| Three Kingdoms | 220−265 |
| Western Jin | 265−316 |
| Northern and Southern Dynasties | 317−581 |
|    Sixteen Kingdoms | 317−439 |
|      □Former Zhao | 304−329 |
|      □Former Qin | 351−383 |
|      □Later Qin | 384−417 |
|    Northern Wei | 386−534 |
|    Western Wei | 535−556 |
|    Northern Zhou | 557−581 |
| Sui | 581−618 |
| Tang | 618−907 |
| Five Dynasties | 907−960 |
| Northern Song | 960−1127 |
| Southern Song | 1127−1279 |
| Jin (Jurchen) | 1115−1234 |
| Yuan (Mongol) | 1279−1368 |
| Ming | 1368−1644 |
| Qing (Manchu) | 1644−1911 |
| Republic | 1911−1949 |
| People's Republic | 1949− |

# A Guide to Pronouncing Chinese Names

The official system of romanization used in China, which the visitor will find on maps, road signs and city shopfronts, is known as *pinyin*. It is now almost universally adopted by the Western media.

Some visitors may initially encounter some difficulty in pronouncing romanized Chinese words. In fact many of the sounds correspond to the usual pronunciation of the letters in English. The exceptions are:

**Initials**

| | |
|---|---|
| c | is like the *ts* in '*its*' |
| q | is like the *ch* in '*ch*eese' |
| x | has no English equivalent, and can best be described as a hissing consonant that lies somewhere between *sh* and *s*. The sound was rendered as *hs* under an earlier transcription system. |
| z | is like the *ds* in 'fa*ds*' |
| zh | is unaspirated, and sounds like the *j* in '*j*ug' |

**Finals**

| | |
|---|---|
| a | sounds like 'ah' |
| e | is pronounced as in 'h*e*r' |
| i | is pronounced as in 'sk*i*' (written as *yi* when not preceded by an initial consonant) However, in *ci*, *chi*, *ri*, *shi*, *zi* and *zhi*, the sound represented by the *i* final is quite different and is similar to the *ir* in 's*ir*', but without much stressing of the *r* sound. |
| o | sounds like the *aw* in 'l*aw*' |
| u | sounds like the *oo* in '*oo*ze' |
| ê | is pronounced as in 'g*e*t' |
| ü | is pronounced as the German *ü* (written as *yu* when not preceded by an initial consonant) |

The last two finals are usually written simply as *e* and *u*.

**Finals in Combination**

When two or more finals are combined, such as in *hao*, *jiao* and *liu*, each letter retains its sound value as indicated in the list above, but note the following:

| | |
|---|---|
| ai | is like the *ie* in '*tie*' |
| ei | is like the *ay* in 'b*ay*' |
| ian | is like the *ien* in 'V*ien*na' |
| ie | similar to 'ear' |
| ou | is like the *o* in 'c*o*de' |
| uai | sounds like 'why' |
| uan | is like the *uan* in 'ig*uan*a' (except when preceded by *j*, *q*, *x* and *y*; in these cases a *u* following any of these four consonants is in fact *ü* and *uan* is similar to *uen*) |

ue     is like the *ue* in '*du*et'
ui     sounds like 'way'

**Examples**
A few Chinese names are shown below with English phonetic spelling beside them:

| Beijing | Bay-jing |
|---------|----------|
| Cixi | Tsi-shi |
| Guilin | Gway-lin |
| Hangzhou | Hahng-jo |
| Kangxi | Kahn-shi |
| Qianlong | Chien-lawng |
| Tiantai | Tien-tie |
| Xi'an | Shi-ahn |

An apostrophe is used to separate syllables in certain compound-character words to preclude confusion. For example, *Changan* (which can be *chang-an* or *chan-gan*) is sometimes written as *Chang'an*.

**Tones**
A Chinese syllable consists of not only an initial and a final or finals, but also a tone or pitch of the voice when the words are spoken. In *pinyin* the four basic tones are marked ‾, ´, ˘ and `. These marks are almost never shown in printed form except in language texts.

186

# Index of Places

Practical information, such as telephone numbers, opening hours and hotel and restaurant prices, is notoriously subject to being outdated by changes or inflation. We welcome corrections and suggestions from guidebook users; please write to The Guidebook Company, 20 Hollywood Road, Hong Kong.